EUCHARISTIC APOSTLES
OF
THE DIVINE MERCY

CENACLE FORMATION
MANUAL I

Read up to p. 30
Schedule p. 111

Eucharistic Apostles of The Divine Mercy

Cenacle Formation Manual I

Bryan and Susan Thatcher
With Seraphim Michalenko, M.I.C.

Marian Fathers of The Immaculate Conception
Stockbridge, Massachusetts 01263
2012

Available from:
Marian Helpers Center
Stockbridge, MA 01263

Prayerline: 1-800-804-3823
Orderline: 1-800-462-7426
Website: www.marian.org

Imprimi Potest:
Very Rev. Walter M. Dziordz, MIC, D Min
Provincial Superior
January 2002

Library of Congress Catalog Number: 2002103560

ISBN: 978-0-944203-68-2

Cover Design: Bill Sosa

For texts from the English Edition of *Diary of St. Maria Faustina Kowalska*

Nihil Obstat:
George H. Pearce, SM
Former Archbishop of Suva, Fiji

Imprimatur:
Joseph F. Maguire
Bishop of Springfield, MA
April 9, 1984

Printed in the United States of America

Mission Statement

The **Eucharistic Apostles of The Divine Mercy,** under the patronage of "the Entirely Perfect Virgin, Holy Mary" of Guadalupe, is a Roman Catholic, non-profit apostolate of the Marian Fathers of The Immaculate Conception B.V.M., headquartered in Stockbridge, Massachusetts, U.S.A.

Our Mission:

1) To profess and proclaim the truth of the Real Presence of Jesus in the Most Holy Eucharist, and to promote, insofar as possible, Perpetual Adoration of the Most Blessed Sacrament and the hourly offering of The Divine Mercy Chaplet for the dying;

2) To bring to a hurting world The Divine Mercy Message and Devotion according to the revelations granted to the Church through Saint Faustina Kowalska;

3) To form small faith groups, called *cenacle*s, which meet;

   a) To pray for and encourage vocations to the priesthood and the religious life;

   b) To pray and work for an end to the scourge of abortion in the world;

   c) To experience the splendor of our Catholic Faith through the study of Sacred Scripture, the *Catechism of the Catholic Church*, and the *Diary of Saint Faustina Kowalska*;

4) To encourage members in the exercise of the Faith through the spiritual and corporal works of mercy, and to help people to become sensitive to the gift and beauty of all life, especially through care for the "lepers" of today – the rejected, the lonely, the disabled, the elderly, and the dying.

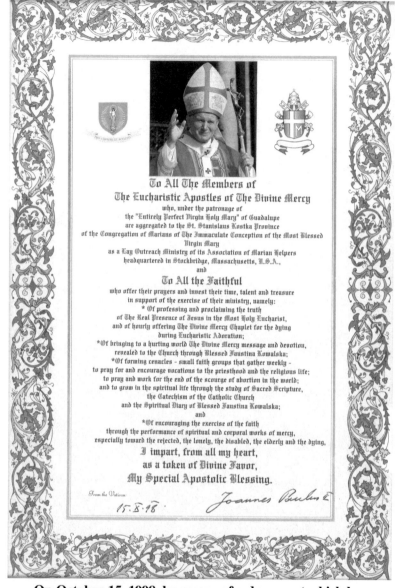

To All The Members of
The Eucharistic Apostles of The Divine Mercy
who, under the patronage of
the "Entirely Perfect Virgin Holy Mary" of Guadalupe
are aggregated to the St. Stanislaus Kostka Province
of the Congregation of Marians of The Immaculate Conception of the Most Blessed
Virgin Mary
as a Lay Outreach Ministry of its Association of Marian Helpers
headquartered in Stockbridge, Massachusetts, U.S.A.,
and
To All the Faithful
who offer their prayers and invest their time, talent and treasure
in support of the exercise of their ministry, namely:
* Of professing and proclaiming the truth
of The Real Presence of Jesus in the Most Holy Eucharist,
and of hourly offering The Divine Mercy Chaplet for the dying
during Eucharistic Adoration;
*Of bringing to a hurting world The Divine Mercy message and devotion,
revealed to the Church through Blessed Faustina Kowalska;
*Of forming cenacles - small faith groups that gather weekly -
to pray for and encourage vocations to the priesthood and the religious life;
to pray and work for the end of the scourge of abortion in the world;
and to grow in the spiritual life through the study of Sacred Scripture,
the Catechism of the Catholic Church
and the Spiritual Diary of Blessed Faustina Kowalska;
and
*Of encouraging the exercise of the faith
through the performance of spiritual and corporal works of mercy,
especially toward the rejected, the lonely, the disabled, the elderly and the dying,
I impart, from all my heart,
as a token of Divine Favor,
My Special Apostolic Blessing.

From the Vatican:

15.8.98

Joannes Paulus II

On October 15, 1998, by means of a document which he personally signed, the Holy Father, Pope John Paul II, imparted a special Apostolic Blessing to all members of the Eucharistic Apostles of The Divine Mercy, and to all the Faithful, who offer their prayers and invest their time, talent and treasure in support of the exercise of this ministry.

Dedication

This Cenacle Formation Manual and Prayer Book is dedicated to Jesus, The Divine Mercy in Human Flesh, whose love for us never ends, and is most present in our darkest moments; and to Mary, the Mother of the Blessed Sacrament. Through her intercession as Our Lady of Guadalupe, may all come to a deeper appreciation of the gift and sanctity of life.

May all who need healing come to the Merciful Physician.

CONTENTS

Preface

The concept of small Christian Communities, where the faith is instilled and deepened in those gathered in an atmosphere of song, prayer, sharing, and fellowship, is nothing new. The early Church started with only twelve apostles and a few hundred disciples, yet converts were added to it daily. *"They devoted themselves to the Apostles' teaching and fellowship, to the breaking of bread and the prayers"* (Acts 2:42). It is stated eloquently in the letter to the Hebrews, *"Let us hold fast to the confession of our hope without wavering, for He who has promised is faithful; and let us consider how to provoke one another to love and good deeds, not neglecting to meet together, as is the habit of some, but encouraging one another, and all the more as you see the Day approaching"* (Heb 10:23-25).

It is appropriate that the Eucharistic Apostles of The Divine Mercy be aggregated to the Congregation of Marians of The Immaculate Conception, as the mission statement of the apostolate is consonant with the charisms of the Congregation and Province.

On October 27, 1910, the renovator of our congregation, Blessed George Matulaitis, wrote in his spiritual diary: "How much good laymen and laywomen could do if they were only instructed and enlightened beforehand in matters of faith, informed about the needs of the Church, enkindled with the fire of holy zeal and then organized into groups and attracted to the work of spreading the Faith! They would be able to bring Christ in to places we priests could not even approach."

The Directory of our congregation acts upon this desire of our Father Renovator in two numbers: No. 84: The lay Christian faithful are to be prepared assiduously for the apostolate... . First of all, they are to be helped to acquire a deeper knowledge of Sacred Scripture and Catholic Doctrine, to nourish their spiritual life and to rightly understand world conditions.

No. 85: The Congregation should take care that the people dedicated to it be joined more closely with it in an association of co-workers, that it may take advantage of their help in apostolic works and share with them its spiritual goods.

The Holy Father, Pope John Paul II, challenged us during his address to our general chapters in 1987 and 1993 with the following words: "Modern society presents new miseries and new kinds of poverty, persons who suffer isolation, families and populations which are the victims of incessant socio-economic and cultural changes, and which are discouraged by the injustices inflicted upon them, to the point that they often lose sight of the true sense and the authentic values of life... You, Marian Fathers... let yourselves be drawn to the swelling ranks of the new poor of various cultures, so as to be able to respond to their deepest aspirations, their thirst for truth, justice, and love... "

I encourage members to be faithful to the mission statement and formation guidelines, and to be the hands and feet of Jesus to other cenacle members, as well as to the local church. Under the direction of the local priest, discern how your group can build up the church, realizing that we are all called to spread the Good News by the way we live our Christian lives. The efforts of the Eucharistic Apostles of The Divine Mercy, to enrich and deepen the spirituality and ministry of its members, affirms our motto, *For Christ and the Church*.

May our Merciful Savior and Our Lady, Mother of Mercy, watch over and guide your efforts.

Fr. Seraphim Michalenko, MIC
Director, Association of Marian Helpers

Introduction

In these pages you'll learn about a dynamic lay outreach ministry that could revolutionize your spiritual life and that of others in your parish. First, we will explain the ministry to you and then show you how through your involvement, the material in this book can assist you in living the message of mercy and an active Catholic spirituality in your home and workplace. Through the effective development of faith-sharing groups, pastors will see the fruits of spiritual growth in their laity through a) works of mercy, b) sacramental participation, and 3) stewardship of time, talent, and treasure.

Why was an in-depth formation program started based on the small Christian community model?

As we traveled across the country speaking to people on the difficulties of our own spiritual journey, it became obvious to us that many people understood the devotional aspects of the Divine Mercy message, but few knew how to integrate the message into their daily lives by taking the needed steps in the conversion process to bring them closer to Jesus — The Divine Mercy and His Merciful Mother. Few had actually read the writings in the *Diary of St. Faustina*, and many thought that Divine Mercy was only the Divine Mercy Chaplet or the Feast of Divine Mercy.

Eucharistic Apostles of The Divine Mercy emphasizes and promotes the concept that the Divine Mercy message is more than a devotion: It is a *Way of Life*. While it is important and appropriate to venerate the image of the Merciful Savior and to pray the Divine Mercy Chaplet daily, if these actions do not lead us to a deeper trust in God, a greater ability to forgive those who have hurt us, and to a stronger desire to be merciful to others, then the devotional aspects have done little to bring us closer to Jesus. In the guided study through the *Diary*, along with the appropriate Scripture and *Catechism of the Catholic Church* references, one will better understand the role of trust, forgiveness, and mercy in our daily lives. We want everyone to realize that this is a message to be lived!

We want people to better understand and spread the truth of God's Divine Mercy and the Real Presence of Jesus in the Eucharist. Under the patronage of Our Lady of Guadalupe, we appreciate the gift and beauty of all human life. We want everyone to understand the daily need for works of mercy, especially with a focus on the marginalized, alienated, and disenfranchised of today: the lonely, the rejected, the disabled, the elderly, and the dying. As the cenacle groups form, we want them to ask their pastor about doing periodic works of mercy to build up the church.

Our primary focus is spiritual development, and all our materials are reviewed by the Congregation of Marians and receive a Nihil Obstat. We hope to form Divine Mercy cenacles of prayer worldwide. Presently there are groups in the United States, Canada, Philippines, Western and American Samoa, Mexico, Peru, Ecuador, Cuba, Ghana (W. Africa), Uganda, Tanzania, Nigeria, Kenya, and Australia, meeting to study the Faith and coming to know Jesus on a more personal level. The Divine Mercy Chaplet is being said hourly in Adoration Chapels for the sick and dying and to magnify the precious gift of the Eucharist. Our cenacle formation prayer books are invaluable guides for the groups as they learn that Divine Mercy is a way of life, and much more than a prayer, devotion, or message. We wrote a booklet on recitation of the Divine Mercy Chaplet during Eucharistic Adoration for the intentions of the sick and dying, as the Holy Father, Pope John Paul II, wants us to spread recitation for the sick and dying hourly in Adoration Chapels worldwide. He has given us three Papal Blessings on our work. Our booklet, "Divine Mercy As a Way of Life," emphasizes the role of forgiveness, trust, and mercy in our lives, and "Living the Message," speaks on suffering, humility, and spiritual poverty. Emphasizing God's unconditional love for us all, as well as our pro-life position, our booklet on forgiveness, abortion, and Divine Mercy is in print.

Again, on the local level, in parishes forming small groups, we want them to meet to learn the Faith and share their Faith experiences. Statistics have shown that more than half of Catholics surveyed do not believe in the Real Presence of Jesus in the Eucharist. Many do not understand our devotion to Our Lady, purgatory, and other dogmas of the Faith. We want to emphasize that we are not trying to turn laity into theologians, but we feel an understanding of the basic tenets of our Faith is essential. We want laity to work with their pastor or spiritual guide to live the Faith through spiritual and corporal works of mercy in their area. We are just trying to build up the Church, one step at a time. Every area has different needs, and the main thing is to grow spiritually and then reach out to others with the love of Jesus.

One of our goals is to spread the Truth of the Real Presence of Jesus in the Eucharist and to get the Divine Mercy Chaplet recited in Adoration Chapels worldwide for the intentions of the sick and dying. On October 31, 1999, His Holiness Pope John Paul II imparted a special Apostolic Blessing to all the faithful who during Adoration of Our Most Merciful Savior, in the Most Blessed Sacrament of the Altar, will be praying the Divine Mercy Chaplet for the sick and for those throughout the world who will be dying in that hour.

Our Lord told Saint Faustina, **Behold, for you I have established a throne of mercy on earth — the tabernacle — and from this throne I desire to enter your heart** (*Diary of St. Faustina*, 1485). And in another *Diary* entry, **Pray as much as you can for the dying. By your entreaties, obtain for them trust in My mercy, because they have most need of trust, and have it the least. Be assured that the grace of eternal salvation for certain souls in their final moment depends on your prayer. You know the whole abyss of My mercy, so draw upon it for yourself and especially for poor sinners. Sooner would heaven and earth turn into nothingness than would My mercy not embrace a trusting soul** (*Diary*, 1777).

For those wishing to assist our efforts in saving souls, we ask that the Litany of Reparation, Act of Spiritual Communion, the Divine Mercy Chaplet, and the Divine Praises be recited or prayed silently each hour for the intentions of the sick and dying of that hour. We will be happy to send a copy of the Papal Blessing to a chapel if the adorers follow the above suggestions. The chapel will be included in our worldwide registry of Divine Mercy Adoration Chapels for the Sick and Dying on the Internet on our WebPages at www.thedivinemercy.org

PART ONE: MAJOR THEMES

Overview of the
Cenacle Formation Process

What is a Cenacle?

The cenacle, or small faith-sharing community, is as old as the Church itself. Our Jewish tradition itself is more centered on a home environment than on large liturgical gatherings. The earliest followers of Christ met in the Temple to give thanks and worship to God liturgically, but met in homes to break bread (the Eucharist), absorb the teachings of the Apostles, to pray, and to nurture the communal life (cf. Acts 2). In countries where the Church is persecuted, the cenacle is still the basic unit of our corporate faith: to meet in small groups in homes, sharing our faith and supporting one another in the journey of faith.

The idea contained in the word cenacle is derived from the meeting of our Lord's followers in the upper room where He celebrated the Last Supper. The Latin word for supper is *cena*. A *cenaculum* is where people gathered to have a meal. Several significant events took place in the cenacle: Jesus instituted the Holy Eucharist there in the company of His disciples; there He taught them to wash one another's feet as a sign of mutual, humble service; on Easter night He commissioned them to forgive sins; and it was there that they received The Holy Spirit at Pentecost equipping them with the power to spread the gospel, the "Good News," to evangelize.

Eucharistic Apostles of The Divine Mercy (EADM) meet in small groups (in imitation of the meetings of the first Christians in the cenacle) to have fellowship, deepen their Catholic faith and the knowledge of the Divine Mercy message, share their struggles and joys in applying it to life in the family and workplace, and to live out this faith together by performing the spiritual and corporal works of mercy. More than being just prayer groups, Bible studies, or service organizations, cenacles are a healthy combination of all of these. They are a way for us to deepen our understanding and experience of The Divine Mercy, which our Lord invites us to exercise towards all others.

Why Form or Join a Cenacle?

The world around us often crushes us with demands and confusion of voices. The mobility of our culture today weakens the family support that many in the past have relied on to make it through the tough times, and to rejoice in the good times. In our world, which is becoming ever more busy, it is important to dedicate sacred time to God and community in order to nourish spiritual values. The letter to the Hebrews admonishes us, "...*and let us consider how to provoke one another to love and good deeds, not neglecting to meet together, as is the habit of some, but encouraging one another, and all the more as you see the Day [of the Lord's return] approaching*" (Heb 10:23-24). What is more important, it is our Lord Himself who assures us, "...*where two or three are gathered in my name, I am there among them*" (Mt 18:20), and thus, we are truly His Body at work, transforming this world into God's kingdom.

Vatican II reaffirmed that God chose to save us not as individuals, but as a community. The message is simple: God calls us to be a people who love and care for each other in community in imitation of life within the Holy Trinity. In all aspects of parish life we want to pray and grow spiritually together, go out in love to one another, support one another, learn and deepen our faith, and reach out in mission and ministry to others not yet in the Body of Christ.

As early as 1975, Pope Paul VI declared that in his judgment small Christian communities have unlimited potential to become a major force in the church in years to come. More recently, Pope John Paul II urged the establishment of small communities within parishes where the faithful can communicate the word of God and express it in service and love to one another. He indicated that such communities, in communion with their pastors, are true expressions of ecclesial communion and centers of evangelization. Upon reviewing the mission of the Eucharistic Apostles of The Divine Mercy, he bestowed upon them his heartfelt Apostolic Blessing, encouraging the development of cenacles committed especially to this ministry of prayer, study, and service. (See the opening pages of this book.)

Our personal gifts and charisms develop and find expression in a more intimate environment, enabling us to bring them to the larger parish or community. As our spiritual life grows, we find that others listen to us, care for us, and God's voice grows stronger within us. "By this everyone will know that you are My disciples, if you have love for one another" (Jn 13:35). Indeed, such joyful small communities are magnets for those whom God is calling to become members of His family, what we call the Church – the coming together of those God called to Himself.

The fruit of ever deepening conversion is works of mercy which EADM cenacle members perform under the direction of their pastor or spiritual mentor. In Adoration Chapels everywhere, Eucharistic Apostles pray for the dying each hour around the world. They visit the sick and feed the homeless. The lonely and dejected of society find that the mercy of God is at hand — our hands, the Hands of Christ. We have experienced the forgiveness and mercy of God in our own lives, and want to share it with others.

Persons who are brought together because they are inspired by a specific interest exhibit great initiative and vitality and fervor in bringing that interest to fruition. A compact group of people motivated by the same inspired goal can assist us greatly in our spiritual growth. The mega-church will not survive without incorporating small groups. Like Lazarus, who was unable to remove the tightly bound burial cloths in order to be free, we need the help of others to free us from the grave clothes of our past. When we share deeply with others, we grow in community and the experience of God's mercy.

Each group formed will have a spiritual mentor and lay facilitator. Under the headship of the spiritual mentor and the lay facilitator, groups of Eucharistic Apostles can determine a common day of week and time of day to schedule their cenacle meetings. In order to be considered an official member of the Eucharistic Apostles of The Divine Mercy, and to receive materials and ongoing support from the coordination team, each member should enroll with the ministry using the enrollment form contained at the back of the booklet, "Becoming a Eucharistic Apostle" (obtained from the Association of Marian Helpers).

Periodically, there will be workshops and seminars available for facilitators and interested cenacle members.

Each cenacle will have its distinctive personality, due to the variety of persons sharing their gifts and experiences. (Relevant insights for sharing are provided in the section about format and guidelines.) Members will find that the cenacles are a good place to ask questions about their faith, learn informally, and share their faith walk with others. A cenacle becomes the gathering where one's spiritual journey picks up speed. Because casual activities, such as potluck dinners, evenings at church for Benediction, or service projects, can also include other family members or new-comers, a cenacle can draw the family closer together and offer others a way to get to know members of the local Church. The "domestic Church" is nourished through active participation in a small faith community.

Cenacle Member Roles

Members — It is important for the vitality of the cenacle that each member pursue and maintain a sacramental life. In addition, a life of prayer is fundamental to a life of action, and so guide-lines and suggestions are outlined in the Prayers and Practices section of the manuals. By taking advantage of the Sacraments of Mercy — Eucharist and Reconciliation — cenacle members will find spiritual guidance and strength for their spiritual journey.

Facilitators – The lay facilitator is the person who has the respon-sibility for guiding the community through the sharing and prayers of the session. In some areas, the facilitator may be a deacon or catechist, but this is not a requirement. It is essential for the facilitators both to develop their own spiritual life, and the ability to promote the spiritual development of the fellowship. The facilitator keeps the fellowship on the study topic with love, understanding and flexibility. Shy members must be encouraged and respected, and extroverted members must be encouraged to share the discussion time with others; creating a warm, accepting, open climate for cohesiveness within the cenacle. The facilitator should be able to help the fellowship grow in knowledge of Catholic teaching and the message of Divine

Mercy so as to integrate these in their daily life. The facilitator will help the different members develop and rotate responsibilities, i.e., keeping in touch with sick members and their needs, preparing formation materials/questions to be shared, coordinating the group's mercy project, etc.

Spiritual Mentor — To help the fellowship avoid problems, and through periodic evaluation ensure the progress of its development, those desiring to form a cenacle should seek out a priest, whether it be the local parish pastor, or another, who will be able to take on this role and even occasionally celebrate Holy Mass for the cenacle to enhance its unity. It is not required that he be present at the cenacle meetings, but that periodically he evaluate the community with the facilitator, discern what works of mercy it should assume, clarify any questions or concerns that may arise, and support it with prayer and encouragement.

Suffering-Soul Members — A Suffering-soul member of the Eucharistic Apostles of The Divine Mercy is one who consciously and voluntarily offers up prayers and physical sufferings to God for accomplishing our mission, encouraged by this teaching of Sacred Scripture: *"Since it is by God's mercy that we are engaged in this ministry, we do not lose heart... But we have this treasure in clay jars, so that it may be made clear that this extraordinary power belongs to God and does not come from us. We are afflicted in every way, but not crushed; perplexed, but not driven to despair; persecuted, but not forsaken; struck down, but not destroyed; always carrying in the body the death of Jesus, so that the life of Jesus may also be made visible in our bodies. For while we live, we are always being given up to death for Jesus' sake, so that the life of Jesus may be made visible in our mortal flesh. So death is at work in us, but life in you... . So we do not lose heart. Even though our outer nature is wasting away, our inner nature is being renewed day by day. For this slight momentary affliction is preparing us for an eternal weight of glory beyond all measure..."* (2 Cor 4:1,7-12,16-17).

Since we realize that these members are channels of great spiritual power and so would be exceedingly helpful to this ministry, we encourage each Eucharistic Apostle to secure the support and prayers of at least one such willing person. Suffering-soul members should be instructed as to the value and importance of their contribution of prayer and sacrifice to EADM. Even though they may not be able to attend meetings, the facilitator shall ensure that their intentions will be remembered by the cenacle during the weekly prayers of petition.

Group Cenacle Format and Guidelines (10 to 15 people)

15 minutes	Song (praise and worship)
5 minutes	Prayers of gratitude (not petition)
30-45 minutes	Follow the Formation Guidelines from the Cenacle Formation Manual – relate the readings to our own lives, struggles, and spiritual walk.
15 minutes	Prayers of petition
10 minutes	The Divine Mercy Chaplet
30-45 minutes	Social time / Fellowship

Suggestions for the Weekly or Twice Monthly Cenacles
Come Prepared! Do the readings beforehand.

1. The lay leader will be the main facilitator, encouraging full group discussion and participation. Established group members can alternate in the role as presenters.

2. The presenter should include Scripture and the *Catechism of the Catholic Church*, so that with time members will better understand their Faith. The discussion should involve dialogue and discussion, and not merely a lecture. It is important to stay on the subject being discussed.

3. Persevere! Attend the group meetings regularly. God will reward you for your efforts.

4. The Prayers of Gratitude following the opening song are prayers of thanksgiving. Prayers of Petition, asking God for certain favors, are to follow the group discussion.

5. Community is built by contacting and meeting members outside of the cenacles, especially when reaching out to others in need.

6. After three to six months of formation, pray and discuss with your parish priest about corporal and spiritual works the group can do, with a focus on the "marginalized" of today, to build up your local Church.

The group members should read the Sacred Scripture, the *Catechism*, and the *Diary* entries noted, and come to each gathering prepared to discuss and share thoughts on the readings. Each should try to internalize a line or two from the above and apply it to one's life situation. As one reads the *Diary of Saint Faustina*, one becomes aware that it is consonant with Sacred Scripture. At the completion of the *Diary*, the major topics regarding the devotional aspect of the Divine Mercy Message, the virtues of Saint Faustina, as well as key tenets of the Catholic Faith, will have been covered in discussions. The lessons require some preparation. But, as members deepen their knowledge of the Divine Mercy Message by these means, they will be able to apply the teachings to their personal lives, and experience the healing of personal wounds and relationships.

There will be supplements for continuing cenacle formation for additional years. They will include additional writings, videos, DVD's and excellent Catholic teachings on Divine Mercy and the Faith.

Note to Facilitators:

• Overly intellectual discussions should be guarded against. Personal experiences of God, Church, and prayer should be encouraged.

• Spiritual development takes time. The spiritual life of cenacle members will not be equally evolved. Be aware of these differences, and learn to address them. For more information on this issue, see the Suggested Reading section of this book.

• The exercises, readings, and communal prayer may not be lively and open at first, but will become more spirited and heart-rooted as the relationships between cenacle members deepen. Thus, the activities outside of scheduled meetings can be very important.

• Be aware of sick or hurting members needing to be helped, so that they may not experience isolation or neglect.

Materials Needed for Your Cenacle
Each member will want to have:
• Holy Bible
• *Catechism of the Catholic Church*
• *Diary of Saint Faustina Kowalska: Divine Mercy in My Soul*
• *Cenacle Formation Manual and Prayer Book* (Volumes 1-3)
• Encyclical Letter of Pope John Paul II *"Rich in Mercy"* (*Dives in Misericordia*).

Show the materials to your pastor, noting that EADM is under the tutelage of the Congregation of Marians of the Immaculate Conception, and that the Holy Father, Pope John Paul II, has blessed the ministry. The spirituality can be embraced and group formed parish-wide; we also have short teachings for parish committees on Divine Mercy, thus encouraging spirituality and formation in all walks of parish life. You may want to ask close friends to start a cenacle with you, and even put an announcement in the bulletin. If the pastor from the pulpit will encourage parishioners to form groups of Eucharistic Apostles, you should have little trouble in getting committed participants.

Overview of the Message of Divine Mercy

This is the initial reading for members of the Eucharistic Apostles of The Divine Mercy. It will deal with an overview of the message of Divine Mercy, emphasizing that it is much more than a message or devotion, rather, it is a *Way of Life*.

Saint Faustina was born in 1905 and was the third of ten children. She had only a third grade education, and it was to this uneducated nun that the Lord chose to spread the Divine Mercy message and devotion.

Having advanced and undiagnosed tuberculosis, St. Faustina suffered much throughout her life. She wrote in her *Diary* on September 24, 1936, "Mother Superior ordered me to say one decade of the rosary in place of all the other exercises, and to go to bed at once. As soon as I lay down I fell asleep, for I was very tired. But a while later, I was awakened by suffering. It was such a great suffering that it prevented me from making even the slightest movement; I could not even swallow my saliva. This lasted for about three hours. I thought of waking up the novice sister who shared my room, but then I thought, 'She cannot give me any help, so let her sleep. It would be a pity to wake her.' I resigned myself completely to the will of God and thought that the day of my death, so much desired, had come. It was an occasion for me to unite myself with Jesus, suffering on the Cross. Beyond that, I was unable to pray. When the suffering ceased, I began to perspire. But I still could not move, as the pain would return at each attempt. In the morning, I felt very tired, though I felt no further physical pain. Still, I could not get up to attend Mass. I thought to myself, if after such suffering death does not come, then how great the sufferings of death must be!" (*Diary*, 696)

Suffering also took the form of rejection, even by her fellow nuns. She wrote, "When the Lord Himself wants to be close to a soul and to lead it, He will remove everything that is external. When I fell ill and was taken to the infirmary, I suffered much unpleasantness because of this. There were two of us sick in the infirmary. Sisters would come to see Sister N., but no one came to visit me. It is true that there was only one infirmary, but each one had her own cell. The winter nights were long, and Sister N.

25

had the light and the radio headphones, while I could not even prepare my meditation for lack of a light" (*Diary*, 149).

St. Faustina drew her strength from the Eucharist. She had a great love for the Blessed Sacrament, and even added to her name, Sister Faustina of the Blessed Sacrament.

But Jesus came to her and gave her encouragement. In one entry she wrote, "Jesus came to the main entrance today, under the guise of a poor young man. This young man, emaciated, barefoot and bareheaded, and with his clothes in tatters, was frozen because the day was cold and rainy. He asked for something hot to eat. So I went to the kitchen, but found nothing there for the poor. But, after searching around for some time, I succeeded in finding some soup, which I reheated and into which I crumbled some bread, and I gave it to the poor young man, who ate it. As I was taking the bowl from him, he gave me to know that He was the Lord of heaven and earth. When I saw Him as He was, He vanished from my sight. When I went back in and reflected on what had happened at the gate, I heard these words in my soul: **My daughter, the blessings of the poor who bless Me as they leave this gate have reached My ears. And your compassion, within the bounds of obedience, has pleased Me, and this is why I came down from My throne — to taste the fruits of your mercy** (*Diary*, 1312).

What is this message of mercy? It is a message calling us to a conversion of the heart. It is a "heart" message, and not a "head" message. In Ezekial 36:26 it is written, *"A new heart I will give you, and a new spirit I will put within you; and I will take out of your flesh the heart of stone and give you a heart of flesh."* The world is in need of a heart transplant; it needs to taste the sweet nectar of God's mercy.

The ABC's of mercy call us to Ask for God's mercy, Be merciful to others, and Completely trust in His mercy. And as He is merciful to us, we are to be merciful to others. The spiritual works of mercy include: admonish the sinners, instruct the uninformed, comfort the sorrowful, be patient with those in error, forgive offenses, and praying for the living and the dead. The corporal works include: feed the hungry, give drink to the thirsty, clothe the naked, shelter the homeless, comfort the imprisoned, visit the sick, and bury the dead.

Trust is the hallmark of those living the message of Divine Mercy. Trust is faith in action. TRUST- T-Total R- Reliance U- Upon S- Saving T-TRUTH, which is Jesus Christ.

Trust calls us to the realization that God is in charge, and everything we do is done out of love of God. Trust is the virtue that is the essence and foundation of those desiring to live the message of Divine Mercy. We are to be vessels of mercy, and how much the vessel can hold and radiate out to others depends on trust. There is much more to trust than believing that God is trustworthy; we must act on that belief and turn control of our lives over to him. Trust requires a conversion of the heart and gives us the wisdom to understand the need to ask for His mercy, be merciful to others, and let God be in charge.

Trust in God is easy when things are going well. However, in times of trial and suffering, doubt appears and we wonder, "Where is God?" or "Does He really exist?" If we pray, discern, and believe that we are doing His will, then we must ask for fortitude, strength, and a deeper Faith. Many of us are so used to being in control, only to realize later that it was God who opened the doors. In times of struggle and frustration, we should have the attitude of Peter, who said, *"Master, we toiled all night and took nothing! But at your word I will let down the nets. And when they had done this, they enclosed a great shoal* of fish; and as their nets were breaking, they beckoned to their partners in the other *boats to come and help them"* (Lk 5:5-7). This attitude requires great faith! However, it is in these times of trial that our Faith is tested. As spiritual warriors, we must *"walk by faith, not by sight"* (2 Cor 5:7).

An important devotional aspect is the Divine Mercy Chaplet. The prayer originated from a vision St. Faustina had of the Angel of divine wrath. The angel was ready to strike the earth, and yet her prayers and pleadings were a mere nothing in the face of divine anger. She began pleading with God with words heard interiorly: **Eternal Father, I offer You the Body and Blood, Soul and Divinity, of Your dearly beloved Son, Our Lord Jesus Christ, in atonement for our sins, and those of the** whole world.; for the sake of His sorrowful Passion, have mercy on us and on the whole world.

She wrote in *Diary* entry, 476:

> The next morning, when I entered the chapel, I heard these words interiorly: **Every time you enter the chapel, immediately recite the prayer which I taught you yesterday.** When I had said the prayer, in my soul I heard these words: **This prayer will serve to appease My wrath. You will recite it for nine days, on the beads of the rosary, in the following manner: First of all, you will say one OUR FATHER and HAIL MARY and the I BELIEVE IN GOD. Then on the OUR FATHER beads you will say the following words: 'Eternal Father, I offer You the Body and Blood, Soul and Divinity, of Your dearly beloved Son, Our Lord Jesus Christ, in atonement for our sins and those of the whole world.' On the HAIL MARY beads you will say the following words: 'For the sake of His sorrowful Passion, have mercy on us and on the whole world.' In conclusion, three times you will recite these words: 'Holy God, Holy Mighty One, Holy Immortal One, have mercy on us and on the whole world.'**

There are many promises associated with recitation of the Chaplet which you will learn in later cenacle gatherings. In *Diary* entry, 687 she wrote, "Once, as I was going down the hall to the kitchen, I heard these words in my soul: **Say unceasingly the chaplet that I have taught you. Whoever will recite it will receive great mercy at the hour of death. Priests will recommend it to sinners as their last hope of salvation. Even if there were a sinner most hardened, if he were to recite this chaplet only once, he would receive grace from My infinite mercy. I desire that the whole world know My infinite mercy. I desire to grant unimaginable graces to those souls who trust in My mercy.** We are to have the Faith of a child, as in Mt 18:3 *"Truly, I say to you, unless you turn and become like children, you will never enter the kingdom of heaven."*

Our mission, as was St. Faustina's, is in saving souls. Many of us fall into serious sin and wonder if God could ever forgive us. Yet we read in Exodus, as God reveals Himself to Moses, "...*The Lord, the Lord, a God merciful and gracious, slow to anger, and abounding in steadfast love and faithfulness, keeping steadfast love for the thousandth generation, forgiving iniquity and transgression and sin...*" (Ex 34:5-7).

Another important aspect of the Divine Mercy message is the Image of Jesus, The Divine Mercy. The image originated from a vision that St. Faustina had on February 22, 1931. In that vision, Our Lord was clothed in a white garment with His right hand raised in blessing. His left hand was touching his garment in the area of the heart. From the heart came forth two large rays, one red and the other pale. He expressed a desire to have an image painted according to the pattern St. Faustina was looking at, and that it should be signed: "Jesus I Trust in You." The Image represents the risen Christ whose hands and feet bear the marks of the crucifixion. Jesus attached many promises to those who venerate the Image. He told her, **I am offering people a vessel with which they are to keep coming for graces to the fountain of mercy. That vessel is this Image with the signature: "Jesus, I Trust in You"** (*Diary*, 327).

On numerous occasions the Lord requested that a Feast of Mercy be officially established in the Church, and Jesus asked that this feast be established on the first Sunday after Easter. There are many graces received on that day, and the Lord told St. Faustina, **Whoever approaches the Fount of Life on this day will be granted complete forgiveness of sins and punishment** (*Diary*, 300).

To fittingly observe the Feast, we should: 1) celebrate on the Feast Day 2) sincerely repent of our sins 3) try harder to trust in the Lord 4) go to the Sacrament of Reconciliation- preferably before the Feast Day 5) receive Holy Communion on the Feast Day 6) venerate the image of Divine Mercy and, 7) be merciful to others in action, words, or prayer. Even hardened sinners converted on that day will receive great graces.

I desire that the Feast of Mercy be a refuge and shelter for all souls, and especially for poor sinners. On that day the very

depths of My tender mercy are open. I pour out a whole ocean of graces upon those souls who approach the Fount of My mercy... . Let no soul fear to draw near to Me, even though its sins be as scarlet (*Diary*, 699).

As Eucharistic Apostles, we want others to come to a deeper love of the Eucharist, and also be aware of the promises associated with recitation of the Divine Mercy Chaplet, especially for the dying. Our mission, as was St. Faustina's, is in saving souls.

The Divine Mercy message is a *Way of Life*. It calls us to a deeper trust in God. We are to be the hands and feet of Jesus, and build up the local Church through our corporal and spiritual works of mercy. In spite of our brokenness, we are to be icons of mercy. We are to receive the Eucharist, and then live the Eucharistic way of life. The Divine Mercy message is one of hope and joy! Let us then, as Eucharistic Apostles of The Divine Mercy, be vessels of mercy to a hurting world.

The Divine Mercy Chaplet and Eucharistic Adoration

Eucharistic Apostles of The Divine Mercy have for their declared mission the foremost purpose of proclaiming the truth of the Real Presence of Jesus in the Most Holy Sacrament of the Eucharist: Body and Blood, Soul and Divinity, as solemnly defined by the Council of Trent, and of promoting Perpetual Adoration of the Most Blessed Sacrament along with the hourly offering of The Divine Mercy Chaplet for the dying, insofar as it is possible for them to do so.

Their secondary purpose is to bring to a hurting world the consoling Divine Mercy Message and Devotion, revealed to the Church through Saint Faustina Kowalska in Poland in the 1930's.

One of the principal elements of The Divine Mercy Devotion is the Divine Mercy Chaplet.

A form of prayer taught to St. Faustina by Our Lord Himself, the Chaplet is significant because it brings together the sacrifice of the Lord's Passion and of the Most Holy Eucharist. This accounts for the powerful effects attributed to its use, as promised by the Savior through St. Faustina, the "Apostle" and "Secretary" of His mercy.

The principal prayer of the Chaplet alludes to the Holy Sacrifice of the Altar: "Eternal Father, I offer You the Body and Blood, Soul and Divinity of your dearly beloved Son, our Lord Jesus Christ, in atonement for our sins and those of the whole world." The accompanying prayer declares, "For the sake of [that is, out of regard for] His sorrowful Passion, have mercy on us and on the whole world," which alludes to the Holy Sacrifice of the Cross. The two most significant moments of our Lord's mission on earth, nonetheless, are in reality two parts of a single act — Christ's sacrifice of Himself on our behalf. The one part constitutes the essence of the sacrifice, and that took place at the Last Supper during the institution of the Eucharist, when with His own hands Jesus offered His Body and His Blood; the other part constitutes the external ceremony, when Jesus was nailed to a cross and died upon it (see *Diary*, 684).

31

The Opening Prayer of the Feast of the Body and Blood of Christ, which is also the prayer most commonly used just before the celebrant blesses people with the Blessed Sacrament at the close of Benediction Services, clearly declares that the Eucharist is the memorial of Christ's suffering and death. For Christians, the word "memorial" does not mean an action of our mind, a mere "calling to mind," or "remembering," but, in the case of Christ's sacrificial suffering and death, it means the making present and experiencing, here and now, of the spiritual effects of that sacrifice upon us (cf. *Catechism of the Catholic Church*, #1366). The Last Supper and Calvary are made present to us at one and the same time whenever we participate in Holy Mass or Adoration of the Most Blessed Sacrament.

To be more precise, however, what actually happens at the Mass is that the participants are taken out of the dimension of earthly space and time, as we experience it, and are brought into the dimension of time from God's perspective. Theologians call this divine perspective, God's "eternal now." Simply put, it means that God sees and acts through everything that ever happened, is happening, or will be happening, in one and the same instant. In other words, all times and places are present before Him at once. Christ's one Sacrifice, at the Last Supper and on the Cross, is therefore eternally present before God, and its effects can be applied by Him to any point of time in history — past, present, or future.

Now, with regard to what has just been stated, what is the significance of the Divine Mercy Chaplet?

Saint Paul's Letter to the Hebrews (see 7:27 and 9:14) assures us that the salvation of humankind was accomplished by Jesus of Nazareth when, through the eternal Spirit, He offered Himself without blemish to God in our place and for us. Through the eternal Spirit, therefore, Christ's sacrifice was taken out of space and time into the eternal now, from where it affects every point of history, past, present and future.

As Jesus entered the heavenly Holy of Holies with the offering of His own Blood (life), He was "made perfect." In other words, He was constituted the Great High Priest over God's Holy Temple, and we, who believe in and obey Him, have been made holy through the sacrifice of the body of Jesus Christ once for all (see Heb 10:10). The result is that He has made perfect forever — that is, constituted as priests — those who are being made holy (see Heb 10:14). As such, in and with Christ our Great High Priest, we are being built into a spiritual house to be a holy priesthood, offering spiritual sacrifices acceptable to God through Jesus Christ (see 1 Pet 2:5). These spiritual sacrifices are sacrifices of praise, the fruit of lips that confess Jesus' name (see Heb 13:15).

As Eucharistic Apostles of The Divine Mercy, then, we need to be keenly aware of what all this means when we pray the Divine Mercy Chaplet. In the first place, our prayer becomes a spiritual sacrifice, the fruit of lips that acknowledge Jesus' name and all it stands for. As we pray: "For the sake of His sorrowful Passion, have mercy on us and on the whole world," we are not begging God to grant something He might be holding back from us, but offering a sacrifice of praise, we are acknowledging, affirming, acclaiming Him as the Merciful One who has in Christ, once-for-all, granted us all that we need to fulfill His purposes for us. We trust in His merciful providence concerning every instant and every facet of our lives.

All the more, then, it is evident, that as we pray the principal prayer of the Chaplet: "Eternal Father, I offer You the Body and Blood, Soul and Divinity of Your dearly beloved Son, our Lord Jesus Christ, in atonement for our sins and those of the whole world," we stand with and in our Great High Priest at the Father's heavenly throne and altar in the eternal "now," and with Jesus we are able to direct the saving effects of His atoning sacrifice to anyone or any situation in the past, present or future!

Christians generally tend to limit the truth of salvation to the experience of having their sins forgiven, whereas the grand, all-inclusive word, salvation, encompasses a great number of blessings which God in His mercy has made available through the sacrifice of Jesus for all who obey Him. What took place at the Cross is what the liturgy calls the "marvelous exchange." The following are the main areas of spiritual and material benefits provided by Jesus for His Body of believers:

- Jesus took upon Himself our punishment that we might be forgiven (Is 53:4-5; Mt 8:16-17; 1 P 2:24).
- Jesus was wounded that we might be healed (Is 53:5; 1P 2:24).
- Jesus was made sin for us that in Him we might become the righteousness of God (Is 53:10; 2 Cor 5:21).
- Jesus became poor for our sakes, that we might share His abundance (2 Cor 8:9; 9:8; Acts 20:35).
- Jesus bore our shame that we might share His glory (Mt 27:35-44; Heb 2:10; 12:2).
- Jesus endured our rejection that we might have His acceptance with the Father (Mt 27:46 and 50; Eph 1:5-6).
- Jesus was made a curse that we might enter into the blessing (Gal 3:13-14).

Other benefits are only different facets of these principle ones.

As we pray the Divine Mercy Chaplet for ourselves or for others, since all the above and more are consonant with the will of God for us, we can be most powerfully instrumental in calling down these blessings on every person and situation or need. Our Lord promised through St. Faustina: "Through the Chaplet you will obtain everything, if what you ask for is compatible with my will" (*Diary*, 1731).

This will be all the more true as Eucharistic Apostles of The Divine Mercy offer up the Chaplet hourly for the dying, especially during the Hour of Great Mercy, and during periods of Eucharistic Adoration. Our Lord urged St. Faustina to do so on numerous occasions. There are at least 35 entries in her Diary dealing with prayers for the dying, many of them encouraging the use of the Chaplet for that purpose. For example:

- **At the hour of their death, I defend as My own glory every soul that will say this chaplet; or when others say it for a dying person, the indulgence is the same. When this chaplet is said by the bedside of a dying person, God's anger is placated, unfathomable mercy envelops the soul, and the very depths of My tender mercy are moved for the sake of the sorrowful Passion of My Son** (*Diary*, 811).

- Say unceasingly the chaplet that I have taught you. Whoever will recite it will receive great mercy at the hour of death. Priests will recommend it to sinners as their last hope of salvation. Even if there were a sinner most hardened, if he were to recite this chaplet only once he would receive grace from My infinite mercy (*Diary*, 687)

- My daughter, encourage souls to say the chaplet that I have given to you. It pleases Me to grant everything they ask of me by saying the chaplet. When hardened sinners say it, I will fill their souls with peace, and the hour of their death will be a happy one (*Diary*, 1541).

- My daughter, help Me to save souls. You will go to a dying sinner, and you will continue to recite the chaplet, and in this way you will obtain for him trust in My mercy, for he is already in despair (*Diary*, 1797).

The Eucharist and Trust

The reading for the group will be the Eucharist and Trust. First of all, any discussion on the Divine Mercy Incarnate must include the Eucharist, for they are one and the same; that is, the Divine Mercy Incarnate is Jesus and Jesus is the Eucharist. Just as blood carries life sustaining oxygen and nutrients to all the cells in our body, the Eucharist is our spiritual food and transfuses us with life saving grace and power.

Jesus is the sacrificial Lamb who gave up His life out of love for us. In Jeremiah 11: 19, it is written: "but I was like a gentle lamb led to the slaughter." In 1 Peter, 1:18-19,"*you know that you were ransomed from the futile ways inherited from your fathers, not with perishable things such as silver or gold, but with the precious Blood of Christ, like that of a lamb without blemish or spot.*" The Eucharist is food for our spiritual journeys and provides us nourishment and grace for our travels on the spiritual road of life.

The Sacrament was instituted on Holy Thursday, and this gift is ongoing and celebrated daily in Masses all over the world. Jesus wants us to partake in this gift as frequently as our station in life permits. "*Truly, truly I say to you, unless you eat the flesh of the Son of man and drink his blood, you have no life in you; he who eats my flesh and drinks my blood has eternal life and I will raise him up at the last day*" (Jn 6: 53-54). The Church teaches that at the moment of consecration during the Mass, the bread and wine on the altar become the Body and Blood of Jesus Christ. The Council of Trent in 1551 condemned the opinion that Christ is present only in the elements as a sign or that Christ is received only spiritually. In John 6: 48-51, Jesus says, "*I am the bread of life. Your ancestors ate the manna in the wilderness, but they died. This is the bread that comes down from heaven, that a man may eat of it and never die. I am the living bread which came down from heaven; if any one eats of this bread, he will live forever; and the bread which I shall give for the life of the world is my flesh.*"

After the consecration, the bread and wine cease to exist although the appearance remains. This change is called transubstantiation. While it is true God is everywhere spiritually, the Eucharistic presence of Christ, that is, that Christ is present Body, Blood, Soul and Divinity is called the True Presence or the Real Presence. When discussing the Real Presence, one can see from John, Chapter 6, that even at the time of Christ, there was disagreement and discussion and many did not understand what He was saying. In verses 48-56, He speaks of being *"the living bread which came down from Heaven; if any one eats of this bread, he will live forever"* and He added *"for My flesh is food indeed, and my blood is drink indeed."* However, in verse 60, it is written that many of His disciples, when they heard it remarked, *"This is a hard saying; who can listen to it?"* And in verse 66, *"After this many of his disciples drew back and no longer went about with him."*

The early Christians who believed in the Real Presence suffered much. There was much persecution and there were many martyrs. People met and prayed in secret and could not openly discuss their faith. As a result, a community of secrecy developed as reflected in the signs and symbols of the early church, ones that could not be deciphered by the pagans due to their complexity.

Early this century when the catacombs were discovered and excavated, several symbols were found in far greater frequency than others. They reflected on the meaning of life and the "Great Secret," the Real Presence of Jesus Christ in the Eucharist. Interestingly, it was not Christ's Resurrection, His numerous healings, the Sermon on the Mount, or the Passion that predominated in the symbolic art work of the catacombs, rather, it was the symbol of the Eucharist that was the focus throughout and was even on Peter's tomb.

I want to mention the Eucharistic miracle of Bologna, Italy. This took place in 1333 and occurred because a pious young woman, a girl of eleven years of age, had a burning desire to receive our Lord in the Eucharist.

Little Imelda Lambertini was born of wealth and entered the Dominican convent at age 9, and was loved by the older nuns. She wanted to receive Holy Communion but was unable to because she was not the required 12 years of age. On the Feast of the Ascension in 1333, the Lord gave her a special gift. While staying after Mass to pray, a Host appeared suspended in mid-air in front of her.

A priest was called and he gave her First Holy Communion. She went into ecstasy and never awakened. She died after receiving her First Holy Communion. Her body is incorrupt and lies outside Bologna, Italy.

One of the most well known Eucharistic miracles is that of Lanciano, Italy, which occurred in the 700's. Lanciano is a small coastal town on the Adriatic Sea. The term means "the lance" and tradition has it that St. Longinus, the soldier whose lance pierced the Heart of Jesus from which flowed blood and water, was from Lanciano. Longinus converted after the events of the crucifixion and was eventually martyred for the faith. At the time of this miracle, heresy was spreading in the church about the True Presence of our Lord in the Eucharist. A monk was having doubts and his doubts were getting stronger.

One morning during Mass, at the Consecration, he began to shake and tremble and faced the people to show them what had happened. The host had turned to Flesh and the wine into Blood. The miracle took place nearly 1300 years ago and is still ongoing. In the 1970's, testing was done and revealed the flesh to be human heart tissue and the blood to be of human origin. The blood had characteristics of living blood and no preservatives of any kind were found in either specimen. So we ponder the miracle of Lanciano in sacred scripture: *"Truly, truly, I say to you, unless you eat the flesh of the Son of man and drink his blood, you have no life in you. He who eats my flesh and drinks my blood abides in me and I in him"* (Jn 6: 53-54).

Another Eucharistic miracle occurred in France in 1608. This unique miracle does not involve a host that turned to flesh or bled but rather, one that defied the law of gravity. The miracle occurred after the reformation and the fervor of the faithful was not as it should have been. In 1608, the services of Pentecost Sunday on May 25 were attended by a full church and at nightfall, two oil lamps were left burning before the Blessed Sacrament, which was left exposed during the night in a single monstrance. The following day a sacristan opened the doors and saw smoke and realized there was a fire.

Efforts were made to extinguish the flames and it was noticed that the monstrance was suspended in mid-air. News spread and many believers and skeptics came to witness the spectacle. Priests took turns offering Holy Mass while more witnesses came to see the miracle.

On the morning of Tuesday, May 27, during Mass and at the time of consecration, the Host descended to the altar, brought in to replace the one destroyed by fire. An inquiry was made and 54 depositions were obtained from priests, monks, peasants and villagers. On July 30, 1608, the Archbishop declared it to be a miracle. Of interest was the fact that the altar, altar linens and ornaments were destroyed and one of the chandeliers was found melted from the heat. Despite this, the monstrance was not damaged. The sworn statements from witnesses are still preserved in the church and a marble slab was installed beneath the sight of the suspended host and inscribed are the words "Lieu du Miracle", i.e., "place of the miracle."

As we live our lives the hallmark of the message of Divine Mercy is trust. We are to be vessels of mercy and how much the vessel will hold and radiate out to others depends on trust. Trust requires a conversion of the heart and soul and gives us the wisdom to understand the need to ask for His mercy, to be merciful to others, and to let God be in charge.

In Proverbs 3:5 it is written, *"Trust in the Lord with all your heart, and do not rely on your own insight."* Trust in God is easy when things are going well, however, in times of trial and suffering, doubt, discouragement, and anxiety appear and we begin to wonder where is God? Does He really exist? If we pray, discern and believe we are doing His will, then we must ask for fortitude and strength and a deeper faith. Many of us are so used to being in control and in charge only to later realize that it was God who opened the door.

Trust is the key; trust is the hallmark of living the message of Divine Mercy. When your faith is tested in times of trial and suffering, reflect on the words Jesus spoke to Saint Faustina:

The more a soul trusts, the more graces it will receive (*Diary*, 1572).

There will be times in our lives when the outcome will not be as we had hoped or desired or prayed about. When we face a trial or suffering of some sort, our reaction may be, "what did I do to deserve this" or, "if God is so merciful, how could He let this happen?" Of course, there are many types of suffering-poor health, addictions, death of a loved one, abusive relationships; in reality, the list is endless. Regardless of the cause or problem, pain is pain and we need to ask "what is God trying to teach me through this cross?" In all walks of life we face adversity. Our Lord told Saint Faustina in *Diary* entry 669, **My daughter, suffering will be a sign to you that I am with you**, and on another occasion, **My daughter, do not be afraid of sufferings; I am with you** (*Diary*, 151).

In Matthew 11: 28-30, it is written, *"Come to me, all you who labor and are heavy laden, and I will give you rest. Take my yoke upon you, and learn from me; for I am gentle and lowly in heart, and you will find rest for your souls. For my yoke is easy, and my burden is light."*

These trials in life give us an opportunity and often force us to question our relationship with God. Saint Faustina wrote, strangely, God sometimes allows them, but always in order to manifest or develop virtue in a soul (*Diary*, 166). That is the reason for trials. Suffering has a purpose as St. Paul wrote (2 Cor 4:17-18), *"For this slight momentary affliction is preparing us for an eternal way of glory beyond all comparison because we look not to things that are seen but to the things that are unseen."*

In 1 Peter 4: 12-13, *"Beloved, do not be surprised at the fiery ordeal which comes upon you to prove you, as though something strange were happening to you. But rejoice in so far as you share Christ's sufferings, that you may also rejoice and be glad when his glory is revealed. "* If we allow it, our suffering will open the door for spiritual growth and a realization of ones total dependence on God. For example, a person with an addiction probably will deny a problem until he hits bottom. Healings will occur through the acceptance of the problem and the realization of the need for God.

When we give our sufferings and crosses back to Him, we live the words St. Paul, (Gal 2:20) *"I have been crucified with Christ; it is no longer I who live, but Christ who lives in me; and the life I now live in the flesh I live by faith in the Son of God, who loved me and gave himself for me."*

Let us ponder the Lord's pierced Heart and call upon His mercy on behalf of sinners, saying, Oh Blood and Water which gushed forth from the Heart of Jesus as a fount of mercy for us, I TRUST IN YOU.

The final topic on this teaching deals with forgiveness. The message given to St. Faustina calls for us to trust in God in all situations, ask for His mercy, and be merciful to others. As God forgives our sins, we are to forgive others of their transgressions. In Mark 11: 25 it is written, *"And whenever you stand praying, forgive, if you have anything against any one; so that your Father also who is in heaven may forgive you your trespasses."*

Forgiveness is at the heart of the Message of Divine Mercy. We pray with confidence to God the Father asking for forgiveness in His mercy as we realize our sinfulness. We pray to God to forgive us our debts as we also have forgiven our debtors. Yet this outpouring of God's mercy cannot exist as long as we have not forgiven those who have offended us. How can we love the God we cannot see if we do not love the brother or sister we can see?

If we lack forgiveness we close our hearts to God's mercy. In refusing to forgive our brothers and sisters, our hearts are closed and their hardness makes them impervious to the Father's merciful love. But in confessing our sins, our hearts are opened to His grace. Yet forgiveness is so difficult after someone has hurt us. We know with men this is impossible but with God, all things are possible.

The pain we carry can be as severe and as deep as a wound festering with infection for years. How can one forgive another after murdering one's family, stealing property, or treating others as animals? Yet even if the aggressor is not sorry, the one injured who harbors anger is the one bound in chains. It is only by letting go of the anger and asking God for the grace of forgiveness that the chains are set free. Think of God the Father in the story of the Prodigal Son who is looking and waiting for us, accepting our pleas of repentance and sorrow. We are to be merciful to others as He is merciful to us.

Forgiveness is easier if we can avoid being judgmental. We should not be like the Pharisees who saw all the serious faults in others but not in themselves. If we could only be as exacting on ourselves as we are on others. Aren't we all so quick to criticize, condemn and judge? How easily we overlook our own faults by justifying and rationalizing our conduct and defects. How easy it is for us to see the speck that is in our brother's eye, yet we do not notice the log that is in our own eye. Think of how many times we recite the Lord's Prayer and we say over and over, "forgive us our trespasses as we forgive those who trespass against us" and yet we struggle with forgiving others. In actuality, many carry anger and hatred for years, never resolving the situation internally. We seldom forgive and rarely forget. Yet we pray to God to forgive us as we forgive others.

In closing, let us reflect on the passage from Sirach 28:1-2, *"He that takes vengeance will suffer vengeance from the Lord, and he will firmly establish his sins. Forgive your neighbor the wrong he has done, and then your sins will be pardoned when you pray. Does a man harbor anger against another, and yet seek for healing from the Lord? Does he have no mercy toward a man like himself, and yet pray for his own sins?"*

O Lord, give us the grace to forgive so we can have peace in our hearts. Free us from the shackles that bind us and help us to become the beautiful people we are all called to be.

Saint Faustina — a Model for Eucharistic Apostles of The Divine Mercy

It was to Saint Faustina Kowalska (1905-1938), a simple, uneducated nun from Poland, that the Lord chose to spread the Divine Mercy message and devotion. **My daughter, be at peace. Your thoughts are to be My thoughts, so write whatever comes to your mind. You are the secretary of My mercy. I have chosen you for that office in this life and the next life. That is how I want it to be in spite of all the opposition they will give you. Know that My choice will not change** (*Diary*, 1605).

Saint Faustina was born in 1905 in the village of Glogowiec in Central Poland. She came from a large, poor peasant family, and attended less than three years of elementary school. When nearly twenty years old, and after a few years of work as a domestic servant working with wealthy families, she entered the Congregation of the Sisters of Our Lady of Mercy. Her seemingly ordinary life concealed in itself an exceptionally profound union with God. From her early youth, she desired to be a great saint and consistently strove toward that goal. It was to this simple nun that our Lord came and announced, **In the Old Covenant I sent prophets wielding thunderbolts to My people. Today I am sending you with My mercy to the people of the whole world. I do not want to punish aching mankind, but I desire to heal it, pressing it to My merciful heart** (*Diary*, 1588). As an apostle of mercy, her mission was to:

1) remind the world of the great mercy of God as revealed in Sacred Scripture,

2) teach us new prayers of devotion to The Divine Mercy, and

3) initiate a movement of apostles of The Divine Mercy who would lead others toward Him in the spirit of a childlike trust and confidence in God, and love of neighbor as expressed in spiritual and corporal works of mercy.

For several years, she was ill with advanced tuberculosis, suffering from much pain and fatigue. Her simple life taught us much about following in Jesus' footsteps. After much suffering, she died on October 5, 1938, at the young age of thirty-three. Her mortal remains lie in the Convent Chapel in Cracow-Lagiewniki, Poland, below the image of The Divine Mercy. She was beatified on the Feast of Divine Mercy in April 18, 1993, and today her name is known all over the world as the apostle of mercy.

Saint Faustina is the ideal role model for Eucharistic Apostles of The Divine Mercy, especially in light of her love of the Eucharist, and her virtuous life as exemplified by doing spiritual and corporal works of mercy. Because of her special love for our Eucharistic Lord, she added, "of the Most Blessed Sacrament" to her name, Sister Maria Faustina. "I adore You, Lord and Creator, hidden in the Blessed Sacrament ... . You have spread so much beauty over the earth, and it tells me about Your beauty, even though these beautiful things are but a faint reflection of You, Incomprehensible Beauty... my heart is completely immersed in prayer of adoration" (*Diary*, 1692).

Saint Faustina prayed the Divine Mercy Chaplet incessantly for the dying, and on several occasions bilocated to the bedside of a dying person. The Lord told her, **My daughter, help Me to save souls. You will go to a dying sinner, and you will continue to recite the chaplet, and in this way you will obtain for him trust in My mercy, for he is already in despair** (*Diary*, 1797).

It was the Lord Himself who demanded, **deeds of mercy, which are to arise out of love for Me. You are to show mercy to your neighbors always and everywhere. You must not shrink from this or try to absolve yourself from it** (*Diary*, 742). One day, a poor young man came to the convent gate. After feeding him some soup and bread, St. Faustina realized that it was Our Lord Himself who had come under the guise of the poor man. After returning inside and reflecting on what had happened, she heard these words: **My daughter, the blessings of the poor who bless Me as they leave this gate have reached My ears. And your compassion, within the bounds of obedience, has pleased Me, and this is why I came down from My throne — to taste the fruits of your mercy** (*Diary*, 1321).

As members of Eucharistic Apostles of The Divine Mercy, we must aspire to imitate the virtuous life of St. Faustina. In order to accomplish this, we must take an active role in spreading the Divine Mercy Message and Devotion which includes leading a sacramental life, spreading appreciation for the gift of the Eucharist and the sanctity of life, and living and doing the spiritual and corporal works of mercy. Like St. Faustina, we may also be called to suffer in this valley of tears. Yet we look forward to being with our Merciful Savior and Merciful Mother, and receiving our eternal reward in Heaven as promised by Jesus: **Souls who spread the honor of My mercy I shield through their entire lives as a tender mother her infant, and at the hour of death I will not be a Judge for them, but the Merciful Savior** (*Diary*, 1075).

The Divine Mercy Chaplet and the Dying

The Divine Mercy Chaplet originated from a vision Saint Faustina had of an angel, the executor of divine wrath. (*Diary*, 474-476). Her plea for the angel not to punish mankind was nothing in the face of Divine anger.

However, at that time, she felt the power of Jesus' grace in her soul, and the words with which she entreated God were: **Eternal Father, I offer you the Body and Blood, Soul and Divinity of Your dearly beloved Son, our Lord Jesus Christ, in atonement for our sins and those of the whole world; for the sake of His sorrowful passion have mercy on us and on the whole world.**

The next morning, when entering the chapel, she heard these words interiorly: **Every time you enter the chapel, immediately recite the prayer which I taught you yesterday.** After reciting the words, she heard, **This prayer will serve to appease My wrath. You will recite it for nine days, on the beads of the rosary, in the following manner. First of all, you will say one "Our Father" and "Hail Mary" and the "I Believe in God." Then on the "Our Father" beads you will say the following words: "Eternal Father, I offer You the Body and Blood, Soul and Divinity of Your dearly beloved Son, our Lord Jesus Christ, in atonement for our sins and those of the whole world." On the "Hail Mary" beads, you will say the following words: "For the sake of His sorrowful passion, have mercy on us and on the whole world." In conclusion, three times you will recite these words, "Holy God, Holy Mighty One, Holy Immortal One, have mercy on us and on the whole world."**

Saint Faustina's Mission, as is ours, is in saving souls. On another occasion when entering the chapel, the Lord said to her: **"My daughter, help me to save a certain dying sinner. Say the Chaplet that I have taught you for him.** When I began to say the Chaplet, I saw the man dying in the midst of a terrible torment and struggle. His Guardian Angel was defending him, but he was, as it were, powerless against the enormity of the soul's misery. A multitude of devils was waiting for the soul. But while I was saying the Chaplet, I saw Jesus just as He is depicted in the Image. The rays which issued from Jesus' heart enveloped the sick man, and the powers of darkness fled in panic. The sick man peacefully breathed his last. When I came to myself I understood how very important the Chaplet was for the dying. It appeases the anger of God" (*Diary*, 1565).

There are many promises associated with recitation of the Divine Mercy Chaplet. The Lord told her to **Say unceasingly the Chaplet that I have taught you. Whoever will recite it will receive great mercy at the hour of death. Priests will recommend it to sinners as their last hope of salvation. Even if there were a sinner most hardened, if he were to recite the chaplet only once, he will receive grace from My infinite mercy. I desire that the whole world know My infinite mercy. I desire to grant unimaginable graces to those souls who trust in My mercy** (*Diary*, 687). **My daughter, encourage souls to say the Chaplet which I have given to you. It pleases Me to grant everything they ask of Me by saying the Chaplet. When hardened sinners say it, I will fill their soul with peace, and the hour of their death will be a happy one** (*Diary*, 1541).

Any discussion on God and dying is a difficult one, as it is a time when we will meet our Lord face to face and be held accountable for the life we have led. It is at this moment of our encounter with Jesus that we will realize the gravity of our sins, and wonder if God could ever forgive us. Yet, we take comfort in the words from Exodus 34:5-7, "*The Lord, the Lord, a God merciful and gracious, slow to anger, and abounding in steadfast love and faithfulness, keeping steadfast love for the thousandth generation, forgiving iniquity and transgression and sin.*"

Jesus spoke of prayers for the dying on numerous occasions to St. Faustina, and also of her mission of being involved in saving souls. He made it clear that trust is the hallmark, the essence, of receiving His mercy. Imagine the number of souls saved, if the faithful prayed unceasingly the Divine Mercy Chaplet with trust in His Mercy, for the thousands dying hourly, all over the world! Our Lord promised that He would grant unfathomable mercy at the hour of death for the soul praying the Chaplet, as well as for every soul being prayed for. But trust is at the core of the promise. We have to have the faith of a child, as in Mark 10:15, *"Truly, I say to you, whoever does not receive the Kingdom of God like a child shall not enter it."*

As Eucharistic Apostles of the Divine Mercy, we encourage a deeper understanding and love of the Eucharist, as well as knowledge of the promises associated with recitation of the Divine Mercy Chaplet. We encourage hourly recitation of the Chaplet in adoration chapels worldwide, imploring mercy for the souls dying in that hour. In *Diary* entry, 1541, St. Faustina wrote that the Lord told her, **Write that when they say this Chaplet in the presence of the dying, I will stand between My Father and the dying person not as the just Judge but as the Merciful Savior**. As God has no limitation of time or space, we can only pray and have the trust of a child in His mercy. We pray the Chaplet with trust not only for those dying in that hour, but for those already dead, and those dying in the future.

The Divine Mercy Chaplet is a Eucharistic prayer, as in it we join Jesus in offering Himself to the Father, in atonement for our sins, in imploring mercy for the whole world. As the Church teaches that Jesus is present Body, Blood, Soul and Divinity in the Blessed Sacrament, we are offering to the Father His only Son, a gift He cannot refuse. We unite with the sacrifice of Jesus offered up on the cross for the salvation of the world. The prayer embodies the Eucharist, the Cross and the love that the Merciful Father and His Son have for each of us. Our Lord wants us to visit and adore Him in the most Blessed Sacrament. St. Faustina wrote: "When I steeped myself in prayer, I was transported in spirit to the chapel, where I saw the Lord Jesus, exposed in the monstrance. In place of the monstrance I saw the glorious face of the Lord, and He said to me, **What you see in reality these souls see through faith. Oh, how pleasing to me is their great faith! You see, although there appears to be no trace of life in me, in reality it is present in its fullness in each and every Host. But for Me to be able to act upon a soul, the soul must have faith. Oh how pleasing to me is living faith!**" (*Diary*, 1420).

And in *Diary* entry, 1572, she wrote that the Lord told her, **My daughter, try your best to make the Stations of the Cross in this hour, provided that your duties permit it; and if you are**

not able to make the Stations of the Cross, then at least step into the chapel for a moment and adore, in the Blessed Sacrament, My Heart, which is full of mercy.

In the Holy Father's letter to the Bishop of Liege, Belgium of May 28, 1996, Pope John Paul II wrote, "I encourage Christians regularly to visit Christ present in the Blessed Sacrament, for we are all called to abide in the presence of God. In contemplation, Christians will perceive ever more profoundly in the mystery at the heart of Christian life."

An Apostolic Blessing has been given by His Holiness, John Paul II, to those who pray the Divine Mercy Chaplet for the sick and dying during Eucharistic adoration.

The promise is that Jesus will grant immeasurable mercy at the hour of death, to every soul praying the Chaplet and every soul prayed for. Thus, we must trust in His unfathomable Mercy in what He said to St. Faustina, **My Daughter, ... your duty will be to trust completely in My goodness, and My duty will be to give to you all you need. I am making Myself dependent upon your trust: if your trust is great, then My generosity will be without limit** (*Diary*, 548).

As we pray the Chaplet of Mercy with an attitude of trust in the presence of Our Lord during adoration, we can be assured that we will be a vessel of Mercy, as we reflect on these words: "Once, the image was being exhibited over the altar during the Corpus Christi procession. When the priest exposed the Blessed Sacrament, and the choir began to sing, the rays from the image pierced the Sacred Host and spread out all over the world. Then I heard these words: **These rays of mercy will pass through you just as they have passed through this Host, and they will go out through all the world**. At these words, profound joy entered my soul (*Diary*, 441)."

On another occasion she wrote, **That same day, when I was in church waiting for confession, I saw the same rays issuing from the monstrance and spreading throughout the church. This lasted all through the service. After the Benediction, [the rays shone out] to both sides and returned to the monstrance. Their appearance was bright and transparent like crystal. I** asked Jesus that He deign to light the fire of His love in all souls that were cold. **Beneath these rays a heart will grow warm, even if it were like a block of ice; even if it were hard as a rock, it will crumble into dust** (*Diary*, 370).

We encourage praying the Litany of the Holy Eucharist and the Divine Mercy Chaplet hourly worldwide for the sick and dying, especially during Eucharistic Adoration, in the presence of Our Merciful Lord. Not only are we to receive the Eucharist, we must also live this Eucharist. We are to let Jesus enter into every cell of our body, and we are to be expressions of His great love. We are to be icons of mercy, radiating love and mercy out to others. Those same rays, which came from the area of His Heart, will radiate to us, through us, and out to a world that is crying out for His mercy.

Pope John Paul II made a special visit to the Shrine of Divine Mercy in Poland June 7, 1997 and after praying at the tomb of St. Faustina, gave a personal reflection on Divine Mercy:

> I have come here to this shrine as a pilgrim to take part in the unending hymn in honor of Divine Mercy. The Psalmist of the Lord had intoned it, expressing what every generation will preserve and will continue to preserve as a most precious fruit of faith.
>
> There is nothing that man needs more than Divine Mercy — that love which is benevolent, which is compassionate, which raises man above his weakness to the infinite heights of the holiness of God. In this place we become particularly aware of this. From here, in fact, went out the message of Divine Mercy that Christ Himself chose to pass on to our generation through St. Faustina. And it is a message that is clear and understandable for everyone. Anyone can come here, and look at this image of the merciful Jesus, His Heart radiating grace, and hear in the depth of his own soul what St. Faustina heard: **Fear nothing; I am always with you** (*Diary*, 586). And if this person responds with a sincere heart: "Jesus, I trust in You," he will find comfort in all his anxieties and fears.
>
> In this dialogue of abandonment, there is established between man and Christ a special bond that sets love free.

And, *"There is no fear in love, but perfect love casts our all fear"* (1 Jn 4:18). As the Church, we proclaim the message of Mercy in order to bring with greater effectiveness to this generation at the end of the Millennium and for the future generations, the light of hope. ...

Unceasingly, the Church implores from God mercy for everyone. At no time and in no historical period — especially at a moment as critical as our own — can the Church forget the prayer that is a cry for the Mercy of God amid the many forms of evil which weigh upon humanity and threaten it.

Thus, we see that the message of Divine Mercy is not a new message. It merely echoes what Jesus said in Sacred Scripture, *"Blessed are the merciful for they shall obtain mercy"* (Mt 5:7). Mercy is love that seeks to lessen the misery of others. And we are to be merciful to others as Jesus is to us. Jesus made surely a demand when He said in John 15:12, *"This is My commandment, that you love one another as I have loved you."* We express this charity through the spiritual and corporal work of mercy, seeing Jesus in everyone we encounter.

Mercy expresses the disposition that we should have toward our fellow men. Our Lord told St. Faustina, **I demand from you deeds of mercy, which are to arise out of love for Me. You are to show mercy to your neighbors always and everywhere. You must not shrink from this or try to excuse or absolve yourself from it. I am giving you three ways of exercising mercy toward your neighbor: The first — by deed, the second — by word, the third — by prayer. In these three degrees is contained the fullness of mercy, and it is an unquestionable proof of your love for Me. By this means a soul glorifies and pays reverence to My Mercy** (*Diary*, 742).

Thus, we are to receive the Eucharist and then live the Eucharistic love and mercy of God. And, we can see that devotion to the Divine Mercy involves a total commitment to God as mercy. It is a decision to trust completely in Him, to accept His Mercy with thanksgiving, and to be merciful to others, as He is merciful to us.

The Constitution on the Sacred Liturgy presented by the Second Vatican Council teaches that popular devotions of the Christian people are warmly commended as long as they are in accord with the laws and norms of the Church. The devotion must lead us to the Eucharist, "the source and summit of the Christian life" (Catechism of Catholic Church, #1324). We are to live our Faith and be the hands and feet of Jesus. We can be assured that He will never save us if we are the people who *"draw near with their mouth and honor Me with their lips, while their hearts are far from Me"* (Is 29:12). We must realize that we are the light of the world. Scripture says in Matthew 5:14, *"A city set on a hill cannot be hid. Nor do men light a lamp and put it under a bushel, but on a stand, and it gives light to all in the house. Let your light so shine before men, that they may see your good works and give glory to your Father who is in heaven."* As we continue to learn the Faith, let us also begin to discern how we can best live that Faith to be the hands and feet of Jesus in our local areas, and to build up our family, our neighbors and our local church.

Life of Saint Faustina

Helena Kowalska was the third child in a large family in Poland. Her mother and father did not have children for ten years, but her maternal grandmother prayed everyday at Mass for her daughter and assured her that the Lord would give her children. After ten years the parents were blessed with a daughter. The birth was very difficult.

After another year, another daughter was born, and the labor was even worse. When the mother was pregnant for the third time, she was quite worried about what was going to happen during labor. She prayed fervently, and Helena Kowalska was born with no complications on August 25th, 1905. The mother said that Helena forever blessed her womb.

Then there were seven more children, but two died very early in life. Helena helped raise the rest of the children.

The name Helen, or Helena, is a name that comes from the Gods of the Sun. Helena's Baptism was registered in Russian because Poland was then part of Russia. It is interesting to note that just to the south of her birthplace was the birthplace of Maximillion Kolbe. One could say that they were born in the heart of Poland.

Saint Faustina was born in a village close to the geographic center of the heart of Europe. It has been said that whatever the faith of Poland, so too was the rest of Europe.

Helena was born to very poor parents. Her father received a little bit of land at his wedding, and on it he and his wife built a little stone house. In the morning, he would work his fields, and in the afternoon he would go around the countryside fixing houses and doing carpenter's work. We are told that his wife would make his lunch and bring it to him wherever he was working, it did not matter if it was snowing or raining. And on the way back she would pick up sticks for the fireplace and stove. She made sure that everything was done around the house. She was not an educated woman, but was very pious and constant in instructing the children in the Catholic faith. As the children grew, she taught them a proper fear of the Lord. The father was very strict with the children, and we are told of a story where one of the sons broke off a limb from a tree, and for it he got a severe spanking that he never forgot.

When Helena was a little girl about at the age of three or four, she was already having visions. She told her mother that she saw the Blessed Mother on top of a beautiful field, and that Our Lady took her up there. The family told her to forget it.

One evening during a family talk, possibly a Sunday evening, her father was joking with Helena. He was telling her things like, "You're not my daughter, you belong to a fellow neighbor down the road." She was so upset and went to get her handkerchief to put her things inside and went down the road to the neighbor's house. Her mother was moved with compassion for her daughter, and went after her. She convinced Faustina that she belonged to the family, and told her that her father was joking with her and that he would never let her leave. This is one of the earliest situations and evidence that we have of Helena being obedient. When she was a little older, her mother would wake up in the middle of the night and see her praying on her bed. "You better go back to sleep to get your rest," she would tell the young girl. "Mother, the angels keep waking me up to pray," she replied. Interestingly enough, when she was older and went out to work the same things happened. She would often get up to pray and would turn towards where she knew there was a church. Later on, one of the sisters said Helena had permission from her confessors to get up. She would turn where Our Lord was in the Blessed Sacrament. So this was something that the Lord must have encouraged her to do from a very early age.

She had a great love of the Holy Eucharist. While people were writing her life story for the official beatification process, one of the questions was whether there was anything in the surrounding area of her birth that would have been a contributing factor in her life. We were not able to get much from her parents, but her father taught her to read at a very early age. He would read story after story of missionaries over and over to Helena, and she would repeat them in the neighborhood to other children. She told them that when she grew up she was going to be a missionary, and the kids said, "We will all go with you!" However, she really had no idea what the religious life was or what a hermitage was; she only knew from what her father read to her. It was when the priest was preparing her for first Holy Communion that she learned what the priesthood and religious life was, and she soon began to understand what the Lord was calling her to.

One day when she was in church for vespers before the exposed Blessed Sacrament, she felt called to the religious life, and from that moment on, she made a little cell for Jesus in her heart, to keep Him company. Her constant desire was to go to church to be with Our Lord in the Blessed Sacrament.

We are told that when she was a child, the family was so poor that there were only one or two dresses in the family. Her older sisters had the priority to go to church so the one who had the dress went to church, while the others had to stay home and help around the house. At one point in her story, we read that one day the father found the kids very reluctant to help out with the farm work. The father said that the one who got up early enough to let the cows out to pasture would be permitted to go to church. So Helena got up very early in the morning and opened the window ahead of time, so as not to make noise at night. There were two rooms and a hallway in the house and all were living there. Faustina got up during the night, climbed out the window so as not to wake anybody up, and went out to the barn. She tied two or three of the cows together and the others followed. Then she took them out to pasture. Her father awakened that morning and found everyone asleep. Thinking no one got up to take care of the cows, he went out to the barn to feed them. He saw the barn door open and the cows gone, and he wondered who could have left the door open. He thought perhaps the cows were stolen and he became angry and ready to do battle. He went out the gate to see if he could see any of the cows. He told this story so well that everyone remembered it, and the children related it later on. As he continued to look for the cows, he saw Helena singing out in the field. He was infuriated and thought she had left the gate open and ruined all the fields. "I am going to get that kid — she is going to destroy all these fields of rye and wheat." He was taking his belt off getting ready for her punishment, when to his astonishment, he saw the cows walking just on the path one behind another in the field with out a blade being disturbed. He was so stunned by what he saw, he thought, "How can this kid keep the cows on the path like this?"

Whenever she could not go to church, she would hide in the garden with her father's big prayer book. She would not come out unless the church service was over, not even when her mother would call her out to her to do errands. If called to help take care of the children, she would not respond. When the service was over, she would come out and kiss her mother's hand. "Mother, pardon me. I have to be obedient to God, and I have to do my responsibilities to Him first. Punish me as you want, but I have to do my duty to God first. Now I will do anything you want me to do." Even in her early childhood, God had first priority in her life; and she would not let anything stop it.

Her family told the story that after she made her first Holy Communion, she was the most obedient of the children. Her parents loved her so much, and they knew they could count on her. When the rest of the children got into trouble, they would get severely punished. We are told that occasionally she would shield them and take their punishment. But when the kids were being picked on, she would complain and tell them, "If you were obedient, dad would not pick on you!" Somehow all the children were very different and had their own form of disobedience. In fact, the people who knew the family said that they did not know how a saint could come from that family. You can see Helena was a chosen child, even from birth. And because of the direction her parents gave her, she made the choice at the right time. St. Therese the Little Flower said that at the age of three she gave her whole life to God, and that she knew what she was doing.

After Helena's First Holy Communion, when people were coming back from church and the girls were showing off their communion dresses and gifts they got, Helena was going home all alone and not in the company of anybody. Someone asked her, "Why are you going home all alone?" She said, "I am not. I have Jesus with me." She was all excited and talked with Jesus all the way home. She did not want to go home with the other girls. Someone asked one of the other girls why they were so happy on their First Communion Day, and she said because she got a beautiful dress. They asked Helen, "Why are you so happy?" and she said, "because I have Jesus in my heart." You can see the evidence was already there at an early age.

As was said before, people wondered if there was an influence on her and the only thing found was something that happened about two years before Faustina was born. The church was having Forty Hours Adoration. The Adoration lasted for three complete days, and one of those days, two altar servers ran home to tell their parents that they saw the head of Christ crowned with thorns in the Host on the altar. The parents ran down to the church.

They started telling people that the boys had seen the head of Christ crowned with thorns in the Host in the monstrance. The word spread around very quickly. The people from the village came, as well as other villages, to see the face of Christ in the Host. They all wanted to see the Face of Christ. The story was told that the crowd was so big and so unruly, that the people broke down the altar rail, broke down the church wall to the priest's house, and broke down the confessional. It was a disaster, and the news got to the bishop. The bishop sent the dean in to make an investigation, and to speak to about a hundred people. Some said yes, they saw the face of Christ with the thorns in the Host. Some said no, that they did not see anything. The result of the investigation was that it was a shadow from the candles on the altar burning that caused the boys to see the Face of Christ on the altar. That was the conclusion from the study. However, accounts of the event lasted so long, that even years later the people still kept coming to this church in hope that they would see the Face of Christ. Nowhere in Saint Faustina's writings or anywhere in the family's depositions was the story recounted. So could Helena have heard about this? A Jesuit priest, who was the premiere Polish historian and custodian of Polish history in Rome, was consulted. He was asked if he thought that St. Faustina had heard of this alleged miracle. He was convinced that the answer was yes. He said that things like that lingered for years, and people kept coming to see the miracle years later. The very fact this event happened in this parish two years before she was born may be significant. It could very well be that having heard this story, she was so convinced of others seeing the Face of Jesus in the Host that it colored her whole life, and gave the direction for her of living for Jesus in the Eucharist.

If we learn about and follow the life of Saint Faustina, we come to a deeper understanding of Sacred Scripture, *"Blessed are the merciful, for they shall obtain mercy"* (Mt 5:7).

Image and Feast Day

The Image of The Divine Mercy originates from a vision that St. Faustina had on February 22, 1931. In that vision, Our Lord was clothed in a white garment with His right hand raised in blessing. His left hand was touching His garment in the area of the heart. From the heart came forth two large rays, one red and the other pale. He expressed His desire to have an image painted according to the pattern Sister Faustina was looking upon, and that it should be signed: "Jesus, I trust in You." St. Faustina felt that the painted image was not even close in magnificence to the vision she had of Our Lord, and wrote, "...I felt very sad about it, but hid this deep in my heart. When we had left the artist's house, Mother Superior [Irene] stayed in town to attend to some matters while I returned home alone. I went immediately to the chapel and wept a good deal. I said to the Lord, 'Who will paint you as beautiful as You are?' Then I heard these words: **Not in the beauty of the color, nor of the brush lies the greatness of this image, but in My grace**" (*Diary*, 313).

The Image represents the risen Christ whose hands and feet bear the marks of the crucifixion. From beneath the garment, slightly drawn aside at the breast, two rays are issuing forth, a red and a pale one. When asked about their meaning, Jesus explained, **The pale ray stands for the Water which makes souls righteous. The red ray stands for the Blood which is the life of souls. ... These two rays issued forth from the very depths of My tender mercy when My agonized Heart was opened by a lance on the Cross** (*Diary*, 299). In other words, these two rays signify the Sacraments of Mercy (Baptism and Penance), and the Eucharist. The Eucharist is the blood of souls, carrying life-sustaining food for our spiritual journey. The water is analogous to the Sacraments of Baptism and Penance, in that through these Sacraments our souls are washed clean. "But you were washed, you were sanctified, you were justified in the name of the Lord Jesus Christ and in the Spirit of our God" (1 Cor 6:11). **Happy is the one who will dwell in their shelter,** said Jesus, **for the just hand of God shall not lay hold of him** (*Diary*, 299).

Jesus attached many promises to those who venerate the Image. As Catholics, we "venerate" images such as the Image of Jesus, The Divine Mercy, which simply means we regard with great respect and reverence the person portrayed in the image, an action which is not contrary to the First Commandment. Saint Thomas Aquinas, in his *Summa Theologiae*, said the following: "Religious worship is not directed to images in themselves, considered as mere things, but under their distinctive aspect as images leading us on to God incarnate. The movement towards the image does not terminate in it as image, but tends toward that whose image it is" (*Catechism of the Catholic Church*, #2132). Jesus said, **I am offering people a vessel with which they are to keep coming for graces to the fountain of mercy. That vessel is this Image with the signature: 'Jesus, I trust in You'** (*Diary*, 327). **By means of this Image I shall be granting many graces to souls; so let every soul have access to it** (*Diary*, 570). Jesus also said: **I promise that the soul that will venerate this Image will not perish. I also promise victory over [its] enemies already here on earth, especially at the hour of death. I Myself will defend it as My own glory** (*Diary*, 48).

Saint Faustina's *Diary* also contains several passages in which Our Lord requests that a "Feast of Mercy" be officially established in the Church, and Jesus asked that the Feast of Mercy be celebrated on the first Sunday after Easter. That day is a day of grace for all people, particularly for great sinners. **This Feast emerged from the very depths of My mercy, and it is confirmed in the vast depths of My tender mercies** (*Diary*, 420).

There are many promises associated with the Feast, the greatest of which is associated with the reception of Holy Communion on that day. Our Lord made the promise of complete forgiveness of sins and punishment if one approaches the Fountain of Life that day with an attitude of trust, and meets the other requirement of deeds of mercy that the Lord made known through St. Faustina. In other words, the grace equals the one we receive in the Sacrament of Holy Baptism. This is not a plenary indulgence from the Church, rather, like a second Baptism, as on that day, as our souls are washed clean again and made as white as snow.

However, in September of 2002, the Vatican, assuredly under the influence of Pope John Paul II, attached a plenary indulgence for those who piously observe Divine Mercy Sunday. This is available to those who follow the normal conditions of receiving a plenary indulgence, namely: makeing a sacramental confession, praying for the Holy Father, and being free from attachment to even venial sins. However, the promises of Our Lord are in fact independent of this grace and have always been in effect for those who observe the Feast.

I want to grant a complete pardon to the souls that will go to Confession and receive Holy Communion on the Feast of My mercy (*Diary*, 1109). **Whoever approaches the Fountain of Life on this day will be granted complete forgiveness of sins and punishment** (*Diary*, 300). The greatness of this Feast lies also in the fact that everyone, even those who are converted that very day, may obtain the great grace of the feast. Our Lord requested that the Image be venerated on that day as well. **I want this Image, which you will paint with a brush,** Jesus told St. Faustina, **to be solemnly blessed on the first Sunday after Easter; that Sunday is to be the Feast of Mercy** (*Diary*, 49). **I desire that the Feast of Mercy be a refuge and shelter for all souls, and especially for poor sinners. On that day the very depths of My tender mercy are open. I pour out a whole ocean of graces upon those souls who approach the fount of My mercy. The soul that will go to Confession, and receive Holy Communion shall obtain complete forgiveness of sins and punishment. On that day all the divine floodgates through which grace flow are opened. Let no soul fear to draw near to Me, even though its sins be as scarlet** (*Diary*, 699).

On another occasion Our Lord told her, **My daughter, look into the abyss of My mercy and give praise and glory to this mercy of Mine. Do it in this way: Gather all sinners from the entire world and immerse them in the abyss of My mercy. I want to give Myself to souls; I yearn for souls, My daughter. On the day of My feast, the Feast of Mercy, you will go through the whole world and bring fainting souls to the spring of My mercy. I shall heal and strengthen them** (*Diary*, 206).

Bringing great joy to all the people, Pope John Paul II fulfilled Jesus' request on April 30, 2000. He declared that the Sunday after Easter would be celebrated throughout the world as "Divine Mercy Sunday."

The preparation for the Feast of Mercy is to be a novena, beginning on Good Friday, including recitation of The Divine Mercy Chaplet for nine days. **I desire that during these nine days you bring souls to the fount of My mercy, that they may draw therefrom strength and refreshment and whatever graces they need in the hardships of life and, especially, at the hour of death. On each day you will bring to My Heart a different group of souls, and you will immerse them in this ocean of My mercy, and I will bring all these souls into the house of My Father. You will do this in this life and in the next. I will deny nothing to any soul whom you will bring to the fount of My mercy. On each day you will beg My Father, on the strength of My bitter Passion, for graces for these souls** (*Diary*, 1209-1229). Unlike The Divine Mercy Chaplet, which Our Lord wants everyone to use, the Novena to The Divine Mercy seems to have been intended primarily for St. Faustina's use. But since she was instructed to write it down, Our Lord must have wanted others to recite it, too. In it, we make the Lord's intentions our own. The wide range of intentions make it a popular novena.

Mary, Mother of Mercy

We know that from the height of the cross, Jesus turned His dying countenance to His Mother, His sole treasure on earth. *"When Jesus saw His mother, and the disciple whom He loved standing near, He said to His mother, 'Woman, behold, your son!' Then He said to the disciple, 'Behold, your mother!' And from that hour the disciple took her to his own home"* (Jn:26-27). In the person of John, Jesus had intended to embrace the whole world. St. Bernadine of Sienna said that in those precious moments, Mary became our Mother as well. While Jesus was praying on the cross, Mary was praying beneath it, with the holy women and John. Jesus' Heart was pierced with a lance; Mary's heart was pierced as if by a sword.

We read of Mary's Motherhood with regard to the Church in the *Catechism of the Catholic Church*. In paragraph #964, we read that "Mary's role in the Church is inseparable from her union with Christ and flows directly from it. This union of the mother with the Son in the work of salvation is made manifest from the time of Christ's virginal conception up to His death. It is made manifest above all at the hour of his Passion: Thus, the Blessed Virgin advanced in her pilgrimage of faith and faithfully persevered in her union with her Son unto the cross. There she stood, in keeping with the divine plan, enduring with her only begotten Son the intensity of His suffering, joining herself with His sacrifice in her mother's heart, and lovingly consenting to the immolation of this victim born of her: to be given, by the same Christ Jesus dying on the cross, as a mother to His disciple with these words: *'Woman, behold your Son.'*"

And in paragraph #967, "By her complete adherence to the Father's will, to His Son's redemptive work, and to every prompting of the Holy Spirit, the Virgin Mary is the Church's model of faith and charity. Thus she is a 'preeminent and ... wholly unique member of the Church;' indeed, she is the 'Exemplary realization' of the Church." In paragraphs #968-969 we read, "Her role in relation to the Church and all of humanity goes still further. In a wholly singular way she cooperated by obedience, faith, hope, and burning charity in the Savior's work of restoring supernatural life to souls. For this reason she is a mother to us in the order of grace. This motherhood of Mary in the order of grace continues uninterruptedly from the consent which she totally gave at the Annunciation and which she sustained without wavering beneath the cross, until the eternal fulfillment of all the elect. Taken up to heaven she did not lay aside this saving office but by her manifold intercession continues to bring us the gifts of eternal salvation... . Therefore, the Blessed Virgin is invoked in the Church under the titles of Advocate, Helper, Benefactress and Mediatrix."

Our Blessed Virgin told St. Bridget that no matter how many sins a man has committed, if he comes to her with a desire to change his life, she welcomes him. She is more interested in the sincerity of his desire than in the hatefulness of his sins. She is always ready to soothe and heal the gaping wounds of his soul. That is why her name is "Mother of Mercy." She said that she is always ready to soothe and heal the gaping wounds of one's soul. Just as any good mother would want to soothe her child, so Mary wants to soothe the gaping wounds of our souls. We all know the tenderness and love we feel for our children. Can we imagine our Blessed Mother's tenderness for each one of us? She looks upon each one of us as her own special child. And as her own Son was crucified, we then became her only sons and daughters. What a treasure to have a mother so full of love and grace, ready to give us all that we need, and to draw us closer to her Son! She told St. Faustina that, "I am Mother of you all, thanks to the unfathomable mercy of God. Most pleasing to Me is that soul which faithfully carries out the will of God ... . Be courageous, do not fear apparent obstacles, but fix your gaze upon the Passion of My Son, and in this way you will be victorious" (*Diary*, 449).

Pope John Paul II tells us in his encyclical letter, *Rich in Mercy*, "No one has experienced, to the same degree as the Mother of the crucified One, the mystery of the cross. No one has received into his heart, as much as Mary did, that mystery, that truly divine dimension of the redemption effected on Calvary by means of the death of the Son, together with the sacrifice of her maternal heart, together with her definitive, 'fiat'. Mary then, is the one who has the deepest knowledge of the mystery of God's mercy. She knows its price, she knows how great it is. In this sense, we call her the Mother of Mercy: our Lady of Mercy, or Mother of Divine Mercy. By her maternal charity, she takes care of the brethren of her Son who still journey on earth surrounded by dangers and difficulties until they are led into their blessed home." (*Mercy of God*, #9 para 3)

Mary is always trying to point the way to her Son, always leading her children to her Son. In her deep humility and meekness of heart, listen to her words in her canticle from Luke 1:46-50:

> *"My soul magnifies the Lord,*
> *and my spirit rejoices in God my savior,*
> *for He regarded the low estate of His handmaiden.*
> *For behold, henceforth all generations shall call me blessed;*
> *for He who is mighty has done great things for me,*
> *and holy is His name.*
> *And His mercy is on those who fear Him*
> *from generation to generation.*
> *He has shown strength with His arm,*
> *He has scattered the proud in the imagination of their hearts,*
> *He has put down the mighty from their thrones,*
> *and exalted those of low degree;*
> *He has filled the hungry with good things,*
> *and the rich He has sent empty away.*
> *He has helped His servant Israel,*
> *in remembrance of His mercy,*
> *and He spoke to our fathers,*
> *to Abraham and to his posterity forever."*

His Holiness John Paul II continues in the encyclical that, "We have every right to believe that our generation too was included in the words of the Mother of God when she glorified that mercy shared in 'from generation to generation' by those who allow themselves to be guided by the fear of God. The words of Mary's Magnificat have a prophetic content that concerns not only the past of Israel but also the whole future of the People of God on earth. In fact, all of us now living on earth are the generation that is aware of the approach of the third millennium and that profoundly feels the change that is occurring in history. (*Mercy of God*, #10, para 1)

The Holy Father writes in *Redemptoris Mater* that, "For every Christian, for every human being, Mary is the one who first believed. And precisely with her faith as Spouse and Mother, she wishes to act upon all those who entrust themselves to her as her children. The more her children persevere and progress in this attitude, the nearer Mary leads them to the unsearchable riches of Christ." Father Richard Foley writes in his book, *Mary and the Eucharist*, that "Many of these unsearchable riches of Christ are found in the sacraments of our Church, especially in the Eucharist. Indeed, in the Eucharist they are literally embodied there for beneath the Eucharist's sacramental veil is the living fruit of Mary's womb. And our faith in His presence then is, in turn, the fruit of Mary's shining faith which in the first place sets the drama of redemption on course."

Given what Vatican II calls the indissoluble bond uniting Mary and her Son, it follows that as Mother of the Eucharistic Jesus, she now remains as closely united with the sacramental sacrifice as with its prototype at Golgotha. In other words the Virgin is present at every Mass with its High Priest and victim, renewing her maternal compassion and exercising her universal intercession. This explains why the mother of the faithful so earnestly desires that we attend Mass frequently and fervently. For thereby we become united in the most sanctifying way possible with Him through the ministry of His ordained priests, makes present before us and for our sakes, in Pope Leo the XIII's phrase, "the memorial of His measureless love for mankind."

Saint Faustina wrote on the Feast of the Immaculate Conception, "From early morning, I felt the nearness of the Blessed Mother. During Holy Mass, I saw her, so lovely and so beautiful that I have no words to express even a small part of this beauty. She was all in white, with a blue sash around her waist. Her cloak was also blue, and there was a crown on her head. Marvelous light streamed forth from her whole figure. 'I am the Queen of heaven and earth, but especially the Mother of your Congregation.' She pressed me to her heart and said, 'I feel constant compassion for you.' I felt the force of her Immaculate Heart which was communicated to my soul. Now I understand why I have been preparing for this feast for two months and have been looking forward to it with such yearning" (*Diary*, 805).

As we yearn for heaven and our heavenly Father, let us put our hand into Mary's hand. She will lead us and guide us to her Son and home to our Father in heaven.

"O Mary, conceived without sin, pray for us, who have recourse to Thee."

Our Lady of Guadalupe

The mission statement of the Eucharistic Apostles of The Divine Mercy calls us to pray and work for an end to abortion, and to help others to become sensitive to the gift and beauty of all life. We want groups to do small acts of mercy with a focus on the "lepers" of today – the rejected, the lonely, the disabled, the elderly, and the dying. Regarding abortion, St. Faustina wrote, "I wanted very much to make a Holy Hour before the Blessed Sacrament today, but God's will was otherwise. At eight o'clock I was seized with such violent pains that I had to go to bed at once. I was convulsed with pain for three hours; that is, until eleven o'clock at night. No medicine had any effect on me, and whatever I swallowed I threw up. At times, the pains caused me to lose consciousness. Jesus had me realize that in this way I took part in His Agony in the Garden, and that He himself allowed these sufferings in order to allow reparation to God for the souls murdered in the wombs..." (*Diary*, 1276).

In 1531 the Blessed Virgin Mary, the Immaculate Conception, appeared on four occasions to a poor Indian named Juan Diego. On his cactus fiber cloak, or tilma, she left a miraculous image of herself. Through the image, she evangelized the Indians about God and the necessity of ending human sacrifice. Amazingly, over the next seven years, all human sacrifice ended in Mexico and millions converted to Christianity! Just as then, her intercession is needed now to end the human sacrifice of abortion, and the mentality of the culture of death.

Our Lady appeared to Juan Diego with a message for the local bishop that a chapel be built to honor God. Twice Juan went to the bishop and was rejected. Our Lady told Juan to go a third time and said, "...Come here tomorrow so that you may take the bishop the sign that he has asked for. Go now, I will be waiting for you tomorrow."

Because his uncle was sick and dying, Juan did not do as he was asked. On December 12th, he took a different path from the one where he originally saw Our Lady, hoping that she would not delay his trip to the village for a priest. Nonetheless, She appeared to Juan on this new path, and told him that his uncle was already well and that he was to climb to the top of Tepeyac Hill and gather flowers in his tilma. He climbed to the usually barren top and found beautiful roses which he gathered and took to the bishop. When he reached the bishop, he opened the tilma and the roses fell to the ground, revealing the life-sized miraculous image of Our Lady.

The image of Our Lady of Guadalupe reveals Her clothed with the sun and atop a crescent-shaped moon, symbolizing her greatness – more than the sun or the moon gods worshiped by the Aztecs at that time. She is wearing a turquoise blue mantle symbolic of royalty, and a rose-colored gown, symbolic of Divine Love. Her head is tilted down as a position of humility, symbolic of her being a servant of God. The black band around her waist and the four-leaf flower on her gown are symbolic of her being with Child. The small finger on her hand is separated from the others, indicating to the Indians that they must believe in the One True God and the Trinity.

The fabric of the tilma usually lasts only fifteen to twenty years. The miraculous tilma was unprotected and exposed for over a century, and is still radiant and beautiful — over 450 years after the miracle!

As Eucharistic Apostles of The Divine Mercy, we promote the beauty of life from conception to natural death, knowing Our Lady is guarding us and feeling reassured in the words she spoke to Juan Diego: "Am I not here, I, who am your mother? Are you not under my shadow and protection? Am I not the source of your joy? Are you not in the folds of my mantle, in the crossing of my arms? Is there anything else you need?"

The Blessed Mother is the Mother of Mercy and Mother of the Merciful Savior. As Jesus is present Body, Blood, Soul and Divinity in the Eucharist, Mary is also Mother of the Eucharist. She leads us to Him and gives us an example of pure humility, obedience, ardent love of God and complete trust in His will.

Mary's life was full of contradictions. She carried the Son of God in her womb and had many joys, but also many sorrows. Reflecting on her sorrows, we recall the prophecy of Simeon (Lk 2:34-35); the flight into Egypt (Matt 2:13-14); the loss of Jesus in the temple (Lk 2:43-45); the meeting of Jesus and Mary on the Way of the Cross; the Crucifixion (Jn 19:25-27); the taking down of the Body of Jesus from the Cross; and the burial of Jesus. Each of these must have pierced her heart like a sharp sword and inflicted pain that only a loving mother could understand.

When speaking to Saint Faustina on suffering and humility, Our Blessed Lady told her, "Know, my daughter, that although I was raised to the dignity of the Mother of God, seven swords of pain pierced my heart. Don't do anything to defend yourself; bear everything with humility; God himself will defend you" (*Diary*, 786). On another occasion, Our Lady told her, "I know how much you suffer, but do not be afraid. I share with you your suffering, and I shall always do so" (*Diary*, 25).

The Queen of Peace exuded humility, encouraging St. Faustina to learn and practice humility. "My daughter, strive after silence and humility, so that Jesus, who dwells in your heart continuously, may be able to rest. Adore Him in your heart; do not go out from your inmost being" (*Diary*, 785). Later she wrote, "When I was left alone with the Blessed Virgin, she instructed me concerning the interior life. She said, 'The soul's true greatness is in loving God and in humbling oneself in His presence, completely forgetting oneself and believing oneself to be nothing; because the Lord is great, but He is well-pleased only with the humble; He always opposes the proud'" (*Diary*, 1711).

Our Blessed Lady encouraged St. Faustina to develop a deeply spiritual life in union with Jesus, encouraging her to do only His will. "After Holy Communion, the Mother of God gave me to experience the anxious concern she had in her heart because of the Son of God. But this anxiety was permeated with such fragrance of abandonment to the will of God that I should call it rather a delight than an anxiety. I understood how my soul ought to accept the will of God in all things. It is a pity I cannot write this the way I experienced it. My soul was plunged in deep recollection all day long. Nothing could tear me away from this recollection, neither duties, nor the business I had with lay people" (*Diary*, 1437). On another occasion Mary told her, " 'I am mother to you all, thanks to the unfathomable mercy of God. Most pleasing to me is that soul which faithfully carries out the will of God.' She gave me to understand that I had faithfully fulfilled the will of God and had thus found favor in His eyes. 'Be courageous. Do not fear apparent obstacles, but fix your gaze upon the Passion of my Son, and in this way you will be victorious'" (*Diary*, 449).

As Mother of the Eucharist, Mary calls on us to pray for our priests, the ones chosen to bring her Son to the faithful in the Eucharist. "I saw the Mother of God clothed in a white gown, girt about with a golden cincture; and there were tiny stars, also of gold, over the whole garment, and chevron-shaped sleeves lined with gold. Her cloak was sky-blue, lightly thrown over her shoulders. A transparent veil was delicately drawn over her head, while her flowing hair was set off beautifully by a golden crown which terminated in little crosses. Oh her left arm, she held the Child Jesus. A Blessed Mother of this type I had not yet seen. Then she looked at me kindly and said 'I am the Mother of God of Priests.' At that she lowered Jesus from her arm to the ground, raised her right hand heavenward and said: 'O God, bless Poland, bless priests'" (*Diary*, 1585).

Mary wants us to think of her as our mother, our Heavenly Mother. "I am not only the Queen of Heaven, but also the mother of Mercy and your mother" (*Diary*, 330). Thus Mary is the one to whom we can turn in any circumstance, trusting in her maternal compassion and powerful intercession. And when we struggle with the stresses of life in situations requiring humility, obedience, trust and an ardent love of God, let us ponder the attitude of Mary, the woman of faith so that we can follow her example of trustful surrender to the Lord: "*Here am I, the servant of the Lord; let it be with me according to Your word*" (Lk 1:38). Then, just as the merciful Savior became incarnate in her, so the mercy of God can become flesh in our lives as well.

My Merciful Mother

O Most Beautiful One
Mother of Mercy and Love Itself
Let your radiant purity embrace and protect me this day.
Let your virginal mantle of obedience and holiness guide me
And let me walk hand in hand with you
and your loving Son.
Keep my thoughts pure, my words kind and
my heart full of trust in God.
Mother of Love, let me treat others today with kindness and mercy
Let me be a light on a mountain top guiding others
to your Immaculate Heart,
and through you ... to the Sacred and Merciful Heart of Jesus.
Amen.

Virtues

This section on virtues has been written to better understand the message of Divine Mercy, and the attitudes and dispositions we should have in living out the message. Ten evangelical virtues of The Blessed Virgin Mary were the basis for the Rule on which the Congregation of Marians of The Immaculate Conception was first approved in the Church in 1699. Although the Eucharistic Apostles of The Divine Mercy are a lay outreach ministry of this congregation, the "old Rule" does not cease to be for us, as for the Congregation of Marians, they are an inspiration for true growth and Christian perfection.

This is the list of Mary's principal virtues based on the evidence of Scripture passages referring to the Mother of God in the Gospels: Most Pure, Most Prudent, Most Humble, Most Faithful, Most Devout, Most Obedient, Most Poor, Most Patient, Most Merciful, and Most Sorrowful. Our Lord wants us to live a life characterized by all of these virtues, as did Saint Faustina. *"In the same way, let your light shine before others, so that they may see your good works and give glory to your Father in heaven"* (Mt 5:16). By manifesting these virtues, we open ourselves more fully to receive, and then radiate, His great mercy. The rays of mercy will radiate out to us, through us, and out to a hurting world.

The Catechism teaches that human virtues "... are firm attitudes, stable dispositions, habitual perfections of intellect and will that govern our actions, order our passions, and guide our conduct according to reason and faith. They make possible ease, self-mastery, and joy in leading a morally good life" (*Catechism of Catholic Church*, #1804).

After reading the writings of Saint Faustina, one realizes what a heroically virtuous life she lived, and that living the message of Divine Mercy calls us to that same heroic and virtuous life.

However, what prevents our spiritual progress in most cases comes from within; pride is the vice that hinders most people. The proud have no need of trust in God, or of humility, since they consider their accomplishments to be of their own doing. Pride retards the spiritual growth that allows us to enter into the inner promised land of peace and joy when God reigns in our hearts. In this short chapter, the virtues of trust, mercy, humility, forgiveness, and obedience are discussed, as well as patient suffering. All are important and characteristic of the life of Saint Faustina.

It is impossible to separate virtues, as all are interrelated. All are connected by means of the virtue of love. When one thinks of charity, one thinks of giving, and this is true because charity is the giving of self to others, for their good, especially for their spiritual fulfillment, no matter what happens to oneself. *"And now faith, hope, and love abide, these three; and the greatest of these is love"* (1Cor 13:13). The supreme example of love is Jesus giving us Himself as our very life in the Holy Eucharist thanks to His giving His life up for us through His sacrifice on the Cross.

Lord, as we read on virtues needed to advance Your kingdom, we ask that You open our eyes and hearts and give us the graces necessary to strengthen the virtues most lacking in us.

Trust

Trust is the virtue that is the foundation and essence of those desiring to live the Message of Divine Mercy. We are to be vessels of mercy and how much this vessel can hold and radiate out to others depends on trust. There is much more to trust than believing God is trustworthy; we must act on that belief and turn control of our lives over to Him. Trust requires a conversion of the heart and soul and gives us the wisdom to understand the need to ask for His mercy, be merciful to others and let Him be in charge. True peace will then reign in our hearts.

Trust requires humility. The proud person, lacking humility, feels accomplishments are of his own accord and sees no need to trust in God. But trusting in oneself and not the Lord will only lead to failure in our service of the kingdom of God. *"Unless the Lord builds the house, those who build it labor in vain"* (Ps 127:1).

The Lord made it clear to Saint Faustina that the more we trust in Him and strive to live His will and not ours, the more graces we will receive. He told her, **Tell [all people], My daughter, that I am Love and Mercy itself. When a soul approaches Me with trust, I fill it with such an abundance of graces that it cannot contain them within itself, but radiates them to other souls** (*Diary*, 1074).

On another occasion He told her, **Let souls who are striving for perfection particularly adore My mercy, because the abundance of graces which I grant them flows from My mercy. I desire that these souls distinguish themselves by boundless trust in My mercy. I Myself will attend to the sanctification of such souls. I will provide them with everything they will need to attain sanctity. The graces of My mercy are drawn by means of one vessel only, and that is trust. The more a soul trusts, the more it will receive. Souls that trust boundlessly are a great comfort to Me, because I pour all the treasures of My graces into them. I rejoice that they ask for much, because it is My desire to give much, very much. On the other hand, I am sad when souls ask for little, when they narrow their hearts** (*Diary*, 1578).

The Lord asked St. Faustina to pray for souls. **Fight for the salvation of souls, exhorting them to trust in My mercy, as that is your task in this life and in the life to come** (*Diary*, 1452). "Today, the Lord came to me and said, **My daughter, help me to save souls. You will go to a dying sinner, and you will continue to recite the Chaplet, and in this way you will obtain for him trust in My mercy, for he is already in despair**" (*Diary*, 1797).

The Lord wants us to trust in His mercy, and when we sin and falter, we must humble ourselves and ask for His mercy. Intertwined with lack of trust in God many of us carry guilt, anger, shame, and lack of forgiveness in our souls. We ponder, "How could God ever forgive me?" In a powerful testimony to His mercy, St. Faustina wrote, "On the evening of the last day before my departure for Vilnius, an elderly sister revealed the condition of her soul to me. She said that she had already been suffering interiorly for several years, that it seemed to her that all her confessions had been bad, and that she had doubts as to whether the Lord Jesus had forgiven her. I asked her if she had ever told her confessor about this. She answered that she had spoken many times about this to her confessors and ...'the confessors are always telling me to be at peace, but I still suffer very much, and nothing brings me relief, and it constantly seems to me that God has not forgiven me.' I answered, 'You should obey your confessor, Sister, and be fully at peace, because this is certainly a temptation.'

"But she entreated me with tears in her eyes to ask Jesus if He had forgiven her and whether her confessions had been good or not. I answered forcefully, 'Ask him yourself, Sister, if you don't believe your confessors!' But she clutched my hand and did not want to let go until I gave her an answer, and she kept asking me to pray for her and let her know what Jesus would tell me about her. Crying bitterly, she would not let me go and said to me, 'I know that the Lord Jesus speaks to you, Sister.' Since she was clutching my hand and I could not wrench myself away, I promised her I would pray for her. In the evening, during Benediction, I heard these words in my soul: **Tell her that her disbelief wounds My heart more than the sins she committed**. When I told her this, she began to cry like a child, and great joy entered her soul. I understood that God wanted to console this soul through me. Even though it cost me a great deal, I fulfilled God's wish" (*Diary*, 628).

Reflect on His words; "Tell her that her disbelief wounds My heart more than the sins she committed." When we confess our sins and show remorse, there is no reason to carry guilt and shame, because He is the Great Physician and can heal our wounds and scarred hearts. Saint Faustina wrote, "Today, the Lord said to me, **I have opened My heart as a living fountain of mercy. Let all souls draw life from it. Let them approach this sea of mercy with great trust. Sinners will attain justification, and the just will be confirmed in good. Whoever places his trust in My mercy will be filled with My divine peace at the hour of death**" (*Diary*, 1520). *"Let us therefore approach the throne of grace with boldness, so that we may receive mercy and find grace to help in time of need"* (Heb 4:16).

Trust in God is easy when things are going well. However, in times of trial and suffering, doubt appears and we wonder, "Where is God?" or "Does He really exist?" If we pray, discern, and believe we are doing His will, then we must ask for fortitude and strength and a deeper faith. Many of us are so used to being in control and in charge, only to later realize that it was God who opened the doors. In times of struggle and frustration, we should have the attitude of Peter, who said, " *'Master, we have worked all night long but have caught nothing. Yet if you say so, I will let down the nets.' When they had done this, they caught so many fish that their nets were beginning to break. So they signaled their partners in the other boat to come and help them*" (Lk 5:5-7). This attitude obviously requires great faith. However, in times of trial our faith is tested and that is when we must trust in Him. As spiritual warriors, we must *"walk by faith, not by sight"* (2 Cor 5:7).

Bryan Thatcher, founder of Eucharistic Apostles of The Divine Mercy, shares his personal witness on the need for trust in our lives. "In November 1996, I had come home from a conference and was very tired. I stepped out onto the back patio of our home and out into the back yard, but inadvertently left the gate to our swimming pool open. Our oldest son called for me to come out to the front yard; when I went in the house, our oldest daughter asked me to take her to swimming practice. In the process, I forgot that I had left the gate to the swimming pool open. About 20 minutes later, our 10-year-old son called me on the phone and said in a frantic voice, "Dad, little John Paul is dead!"

John Paul was 18 months old at the time and was the fruit of a healed marriage. John Paul was a joy in our hearts and the apple of my eyes. I could not believe what I was hearing. I was told that John Paul was blue and not breathing; my wife had found him floating in the pool, as someone had left the pool gate open. I told our son to call the emergency squad and to have mother start resuscitation. As I drove home with our daughters, I began crying and praying to God, our Blessed Mother, and all the saints. I pleaded for all in heaven to intercede and for Jesus, The Divine Mercy to have pity on John Paul. I realized that at this point in my life what I needed most was trust. As a Eucharistic Apostle, I had been talking and traveling and speaking on Divine Mercy and trust, and yet that was what I needed most of all. The Scripture verse that came to my mind was the story of Abraham offering Isaac up to God. And like Abraham, who offered Isaac to the Father, I said to Jesus, "He's yours, I am giving him back. I thank you for the time you have given him to us. I realize what a great gift John Paul is, but he is Yours, and I give him back." I finished the drive home not knowing what I would find. As I turned the corner to our home, the emergency squad arrived. They rushed a semi-comatose John Paul to the intensive care unit. All of our family went to the hospital, and I called my sister and asked her to pray for John Paul at her prayer group that night. Over the next 24 hours, John Paul's mental clarity and orientation improved, and within 36 hours he was released, totally normal.

Three weeks later, I saw my sister for the holidays. She said to me, "I haven't had a chance to tell you this story. We prayed for John Paul in prayer group that night, and the following morning a member called and said that she knew John Paul would be fine. While praying the following morning, she had a vision of Abraham offering Isaac up to God, and Jesus stepped in the middle and gave him back!"

I looked at her and said, "Let me tell you the rest of the story!"

The episode also gave me a deeper appreciation of the gift of life. I now better recognize the fragility of life and the fact that God does not promise us tomorrow. I try to take things more on a day-to-day basis, realizing that God is in control.

God has blessed me with a beautiful wife and family. Whether any of us will be here tomorrow is of little significance, as I realize that I must enjoy them today. When you are facing trial and adversity in your life, trust in the Lord with all your might, regardless of the outcome. He will pour His abundant graces upon you, and give you the strength to get through any difficulty.

O Lord, touch our souls and let Your Divine Light put our hearts on fire. Help us realize that only by trusting You and putting our lives in Your hands can we understand true peace, the peace that only You can give.

Humility

Humility is the virtue recognizing dependence on God, and one most pleasing to God. It is one of the ten evangelical virtues of the Blessed Virgin Mary. On the Feast of The Immaculate Conception, Saint Faustina saw the Blessed Mother who said to her, "'I desire, my dearly beloved daughter, that you practice the three virtues that are dearest to me – and most pleasing to God. The first is humility, humility, and once again humility; the second virtue, purity; the third virtue, love of God. As my daughter, you must especially radiate with these virtues.' When the conversation ended, she pressed me to her heart and disappeared" (*Diary*, 1415). In contrast to a humble person, a proud person believes accomplishments are a result of his own efforts and fails to see them as a gift from God. Saint Faustina wrote "humility, humility, and ever humility, as we can do nothing of ourselves; all is purely and simply God's grace" (*Diary*, 55).

The Blessed Mother gave a beautiful example of humility at the Incarnation when she replied, "*Here am I, the servant of the Lord; let it be with me according to Your word*" (Lk 1:38). While Mary wondered how all this could be as she had no husband, she recognized God's will. She did not answer with false humility saying, "I could never do that as I am not worthy," but instead, with true humility, gave a "Yes!" for she realized that it was God's plan, and that with God all things are possible.

The humble person also avoids being judgmental, as he knows he is a sinner and everything good comes from God. Saint Faustina wrote, "I must never judge anyone, but look at others with leniency and at myself with severity. I must refer everything to God" (*Diary*, 253). Scripture says "*Do not judge, so that you may not be judged. For with the judgment you make you will be judged, and the measure you give will be the measure you get. Why do you see the speck in your neighbor's eye, but do not notice the log in your own eye?*" (Mt 7:1-3).

How easy it is for us to always criticize and condemn others and how easily we overlook our own glaring faults. Ironically, God often uses the weakest to carry His message, as the repentant sinner recognizes his shortcomings and is more on fire for the Lord.

"During a meditation on humility, an old doubt returned: that a soul as miserable as mine could not carry out the task which the Lord was demanding [of me]. Just as I was analyzing this doubt, the priest who was conducting the retreat interrupted his train of thought and spoke about the very thing I was having doubts about; namely, that God usually chooses the weakest and simplest souls as tools for His greatest works; that we can see that this is an undeniable truth when we look at the men He chose to be His apostles; or again, when we look at the history of the Church and see what great works were done by souls that were the least capable of accomplishing them; for it is just in this way that God's works are revealed for what they are, the works of God. When my doubt had completely disappeared, the priest resumed his conference on humility" (*Diary*, 464).

Paul wrote, "*Consider your own call, brothers and sisters: not many of you were wise by human standards, not many were powerful, not many were of noble birth. But God chose what is foolish in the world to shame the wise; God chose what is weak in the world to shame the strong; God chose what is low and despised in the world, things that are not, to reduce to nothing things that are, so that no one might boast in the presence of God. He is the source of your life in Christ Jesus, who became for us wisdom from God, and righteousness and sanctification and redemption, in order that as it is written, 'Let the one who boasts, boast in the Lord*'" (1 Cor 1:26-31).

The humble person is in the world but not part of it; he has detachment from worldly things and recognizes that the lasting pearl is the kingdom of God. Our Lord spoke on this to St. Faustina and said, **Today, penetrate into the spirit of My poverty and arrange everything in such a way that the most destitute will have no reason to envy you. I find pleasure not in large buildings and magnificent structures, but in a pure and humble heart** (*Diary*, 532). "*God opposes the proud, but gives grace to the humble*" (Jas 4:6).

We are called to do all things with a humble and contrite heart. St. John the Baptist said, "He must increase but I must decrease" (Jn 3:30). As we become more aware of our failings and shortcomings, we need only pray, "*Lord I am not worthy to have You come under my roof*" (Mt 8:8).

Forgiveness

The message given to Saint Faustina calls for us to trust in God in all situations, ask for His mercy, and be merciful to others. As God forgives our sins, we are to forgive others of transgressions. *"Whenever you stand praying, forgive, if you have anything against anyone; so that your Father in heaven may also forgive you your trespasses"* (Mk 11:25).

Forgiveness is at the heart of the message of Divine Mercy. We pray with confidence to God the Father, asking for His forgiveness and mercy, as we realize our sinfulness. And we pray, *"And forgive us our debts, as we also have forgiven our debtors"* (Mt 6:12). This outpouring of God's mercy cannot be received as long as we have not forgiven those who have offended us. How can we love the God we cannot see, if we do not love the brother or sister we can see? If we lack forgiveness, we close our hearts to God's mercy. In refusing to forgive our brothers and sisters, our hearts are closed and their hardness makes them impervious to the Father's merciful love; but in confessing our sins, our hearts are opened to his grace (cf. *Catechism of the Catholic Church*, #2840).

Forgiveness is so difficult after someone has hurt us! Yet, *"For mortals it is impossible, but for God all things are possible"* (Mt 19:26). The pain we carry can be as severe and as deep as a wound festering with infection for years. How could one forgive another who has murdered one's family, stolen property, or treated others as animals? Yet, even if the aggressor is not sorry, the one injured who harbors anger is the one bound in chains. It is only by letting go of the anger and asking God for the grace of forgiveness that the chains are broken, and we are set free.

God Our Father, as in the story of the prodigal son (Lk 15:11-32), is looking and waiting for us, accepting our pleas of repentance and sorrow. We are to be merciful to others as He is merciful to us. Jesus told St. Faustina on one occasion during Eucharistic adoration, **These rays of mercy will pass through you, just as they have passed through this Host, and they will go out through all the world** (*Diary*, 441). She wrote on June 20, 1937, "We resemble God most when we forgive our neighbors" (*Diary,* 1148). Forgiveness means more than avoiding interaction with those who have hurt us. Scripture is clear that as our Heavenly Father loves us, we are to love others. *"You shall not take vengeance or bear any grudge against any of your people, but you shall love your neighbor as yourself: I am the Lord"* (Lev 19:18). We should have the attitude of Christ, who while suffering on the cross for us, said, *"Father, forgive them; for they do not know what they are doing"* (Lk 23:34).

Forgiveness is easier if we can avoid being judgmental. We should not be like the Pharisees, who saw all the serious faults in others but not in themselves. If we could only be as exacting on ourselves as we are on others! Aren't we all so quick to criticize, condemn and judge? How easily we overlook our own faults by justifying and rationalizing our conduct and defects. *"Why do you see the speck in your neighbor's eye, but do not notice the log in your own eye?* (Mt 7:3).

Many carry anger and guilt for years, only to see unresolved issues manifested as aberrant behavior in the form of negativism, outbursts of violence, and addictive behaviors. Many turn to alcohol, drugs, or the pleasures of the flesh for relief of pain. Yet only Jesus can bring everlasting peace. If we are to be icons of mercy, we must be as serene as a calm lake, reflecting His rays of love and mercy. Forgiveness of those who have hurt us will help calm our troubled waters.

Think of how many times we as Christians recite the Lord's Prayer! We say over and over, "Forgive us our trespasses as we forgive those who trespass against us," and yet we struggle with forgiving others. In actuality, many carry anger and hatred for years, never resolving the situation internally. We seldom forgive and rarely forget, and yet we pray for God to forgive us as we forgive others.

Reflect on the passage: *"The vengeful will face the Lord's vengeance, for he keeps a strict account of their sins. Forgive your neighbor the wrong he had done, and then your sins will be pardoned when you pray. Does anyone harbor anger against another, and expect healing from the Lord? If one has no mercy toward another like himself, can he then seek pardon for his own sins?"* (Sir 28:1-4).

O Lord, give us the grace to forgive so we can have peace in our hearts. Free us from the shackles that bind us, and help us become people who radiate Your mercy to others.

Obedience

Obedience for laity is different and perhaps more difficult than for religious, as we do not take vows of obedience to a superior. We are called to be obedient to Holy Mother Church and to do the will of God, which can at times be difficult to discern. We should be like Jesus who took all things to prayer. We need to strive for purity of intention in decisions, and through prayer God's will becomes apparent if we can listen to the gentle whispers of the Spirit.

Frequently we find ourselves involved in various committees and community boards and pulled in many directions. Through prayer we can better discern God's will and reflect on our motives: Is it my pride that I do all these things, or is it God's will?

Saint Faustina was always obedient, even if it involved humiliation. The Lord also emphasized that obedience means more to Him than sacrifice or burnt offerings. He told her, **My daughter, you please Me more by ... obedience and love of Me than by fasting and mortifying yourself of your own will. A soul that loves Me very much must, ought to live by My will. I know your heart, and I know that it will not be satisfied by anything but My love alone** (*Diary*, 1023).

On one occasion, Faustina was told by her confessor of the need to be obedient. Later she wrote, "I became absorbed in prayer and said my penance. Then I suddenly saw the Lord, who said to me, **My daughter, know that you give greater glory by a single act of obedience than by long prayers and mortifications**. Oh, how good it is to live under obedience, to live conscious of the fact that everything I do is pleasing to God!" (*Diary*, 894).

Obedience means not seeing our will as paramount, but recognizing and doing the will of God. When the Sadducees and priests told John and Peter not to speak or teach in the name of Jesus, they knew what they had to do. But Peter and John answered them, "*Whether it is right in God's sight to listen to you rather than to God, you must judge; for we cannot keep from speaking about what we have seen and heard"* (Acts 4:19-20).

The ultimate example of obedience comes from the Lord, *"And being found in human form, He humbled himself and became obedient to the point of death, even death on a cross"* (Phil 2:8). Reflect on the bitter and painful Passion and the obedience of Christ to the will of the Father. Imagine His deep sorrow when He prayed, *"My Father, if it is possible, let this cup pass from Me; yet not what I want but what you want"* (Mt 26:39).

Even as a child, Jesus was obedient to Joseph and Mary. *"And He went down with them and came to Nazareth, and was obedient to them"* (Lk 2:51). Scripture is filled with beautiful passages on the necessity of obedience to parents. In Sirach 3:1-9 it is written, *"Listen to Me, your Father, O children; and act accordingly, that you may be kept in safety. For the Lord honored the Father above the children, and He confirmed the right of the mother over her sons. Whoever honors his Father atones for sins and whoever glorifies his mother is like one who lays up treasure. Whoever honors his father will be gladdened by his own children, and when he prays he will be heard. Whoever glorifies his father will have long life, and whoever obeys the Lord will refresh his mother; he will serve his parents as his masters. Honor your father by word and deed, that a blessing from him may come upon you. For a father's blessing strengthens the houses of the children, but a mother's curse uproots their foundations"* (Sir 3:1-9). And in Ephesians 6:14, *"Children, obey your parents in the Lord, for this is right. Honor your father and your mother, (this is the first commandment with a promise), that it may be well with you and that you may live long on the earth. Fathers, do not provoke your children to anger, but bring them up in the discipline and instruction of the Lord."*

Obedience to Holy Mother Church is necessary, even if we disagree with a particular church teaching. In that situation, we should pray for the grace of understanding and acceptance. *"For we walk by faith, not by sight"* (2 Cor 5:7). We should ask *our Lord to take the scales off our eyes so we can believe, for "In the path of righteousness there is life, in walking its path there is no death"* (Prov 12:28).

Obedience is more pleasing to God than sacrifice, and we need to pray earnestly for wisdom and strength to live in His will and not our own will. Just as our Lord came to do the will of the Father, we must be obedient and try to do only the Lord's will. Jesus told Saint Faustina, **Yes, when you are obedient I take away your weakness and replace it with My strength. I am very surprised that souls do not want to make that exchange with Me** (*Diary,* 381).

In summary, discernment through prayer as to God's will is essential if we are to be obedient. He values obedience more than sacrifice or offering. May we learn through prayer and the gentle whispers of the Holy Spirit what His will is for us in our lives.

Come Holy Spirit

Come, Holy Spirit.
Let me listen instead of doing all the talking.
Replace my anxiety with a calm confidence and my fear with a deeper faith.
Give me the grace to follow your prompting and to do Your will and not mine.
Give me Your gifts of knowledge, counsel and wisdom and
Take away my fear, anxiety, shame and self-doubt.
Let me live in You and You in me.
Amen.

Mercy

After considering the virtues, tet us reflect on God's mercy and what he told St. Faustina, **My daughter, do you think that you have written enough about My mercy? What you have written is but a drop compared to the ocean. I am Love and Mercy itself. There is no misery that could be a match for My mercy, neither will misery exhaust it, because as it is being granted — it in-creases. The soul that trusts in My mercy is most fortunate, because I Myself take care of it** (*Diary*, 1273).

Mercy is love that seeks to forgive, console, assist, and care for others in time of need. Mercy is an act of love done without expecting anything in return; it is done for love itself. Our Lord gave of Himself on Holy Thursday when He instituted the Most Blessed Sacrament; the Eucharist perpetuates this act of self-giving occurring daily on altars throughout the world.

Jesus made it clear in Sacred Scripture that love of God and neighbor is the greatest commandment: "*But when the Pharisees heard that He had silenced the Sadducees, they came together. And one of them, a lawyer, asked Him a question, to test Him. 'Teacher, what is the great commandment in the law?' And He said to him, 'You shall love the Lord your God with all your heart, and with all your soul, with all your mind. This is the great and first commandment. And a second is like it: You shall love your neighbor as yourself. On these two commandments depend all the law and the prophets'*" (Mt 22: 34-40).

Our Lord wants us both to know of His unfathomable mercy, and to be merciful to others, as He is merciful to us. Jesus told Saint Faustina: **Proclaim that mercy is the greatest attribute of God. All the works of My hands are crowned with mercy** (*Diary*, 301).

Imagine the love and pity our Lord had for the repentant sinner Mary Magdalene. He read her heart and knew how penitent she was, much more so than the self-righteous Pharisees who thought that the Kingdom of God belonged to them because of their social status. "*Because this people draws near with their mouths and honors Me with their lips, while their hearts are far from Me*" (Is 29:13). And when we sin, He wants us to humble ourselves, coming back to Him, and asking for forgiveness. He told St. Faustina, **The greater the sinner, the greater the right he has to My mercy. My mercy is confirmed in every work of My hands. He who trusts in My mercy will not perish, for all his affairs are Mine, and his enemies will be shattered at the base of My footstool** (*Diary*, 723).

The Lord wants us to return to Him with humility. *"For the Lord your God is gracious and merciful, and will not turn away His face from you, if you return to Him"* (2 Chr 30:9). *"Yet even now, says the Lord, return to Me with all your heart, with fasting, with weeping, and with mourning; and rend your hearts and not your garments"* (Joel 2:12).

Many of us fall into a downhill spiral of sin and guilt, believing we could never be forgiven, let alone approach God because of our pathetic wretchedness and sinfulness. But Jesus shared meals with tax collectors and prostitutes, saying, *"I have not come to call the righteous, but sinners to repentance"* (Lk 5:32). He told St. Faustina that He is ready to grant graces to souls, but few are willing to accept them:

My Heart overflows with great mercy for souls, and especially for poor sinners. If only they could understand that I am the best of Fathers to them and that it is for them that the Blood and Water flowed from My heart as from a fount overflowing with mercy (*Diary*, 367).

And as in the parable of the prodigal son, the Lord will always take us back with open arms: *"But when the goodness and loving kindness of God our Savior appeared, he saved us, not because of deeds done by us in righteousness, but in virtue of his own mercy, by the washing of regeneration and renewal in the Holy Spirit"* (Tit 3:4-5).

Can we love God without forgiving, loving, and being merciful to our neighbor? Scripture is clear on this, *"If anyone says, 'I love God,' and hates his brother, he is a liar; for whoever does not love his brother whom he has seen, cannot love God whom he has not seen"* (1 Jn 5:20). We are to be merciful to others just as we are to ask for His mercy. *"Be merciful even as your Father is merciful"* (Lk 6:36). This can be accomplished in a number of ways. Saint Faustina wrote, "For there are three ways of performing an act of mercy: The merciful word, by forgiving and by comforting; secondly, if you can offer no word, then pray — that too is mercy; and thirdly, deeds of mercy" (*Diary*, 1158).

At any point in time, we may not be able to say a merciful word or perform a deed of mercy, but prayer is within the grasp of every soul. And when we perform deeds of mercy, we should strive to see Jesus in our fellow man. Saint Faustina recognized her shortcomings and prayed that she would be a reflection of His great mercy. She wrote:

Help me, O Lord, that my eyes may be merciful, so that I may never suspect or judge from appearances, but look for what is beautiful in my neighbors' souls and come to their rescue. Help me, that my ears may be merciful, so that I may give heed to my neighbors' needs and not be indifferent to their pains and moanings. Help me, O Lord, that my tongue may be merciful, so that I should never speak negatively of my neighbor, but have a word of comfort and forgiveness for all. Help me, O Lord, that my hands may be merciful and filled with good deeds, so that I may do only good to my neighbors and take upon myself the more difficult and toilsome tasks. Help me, that my feet may be merciful, so that I may hurry to assist my neighbor, overcoming my own fatigue and weariness. My true rest is in the service of my neighbor. Help me, O Lord, that my heart may be merciful so that I myself may feel all the sufferings of my neighbor. I will refuse my heart to no one. I will be sincere even with those who, I know, will abuse my kindness. And I will lock myself up in the most merciful Heart of Jesus. I will bear my own suffering in silence. May Your mercy, O Lord, rest upon me.

(*Diary*, 163)

The ministry of Eucharistic Apostles of The Divine Mercy involves corporal works of mercy projects all over the world, and people often say to me, "I wish I could do such great things!" They marvel at the containers of medical supplies, wheelchairs, clothing, and religious articles that we ship to the poorest of the poor. And in many ways it is amazing. But most don't realize that it is the little things in life, done out of great love for God, that are most pleasing to Him. It is much easier to box children's shoes for Africa than it is to be merciful to a teenage son who is breaking every rule in the house! It is much easier to visit an unknown AIDS victim in the hospital than it is to be merciful to a pregnant unwed daughter. Few are called to travel to far away places and evangelize; but all are called to be witnesses and evangelists in our own family and workplace!

Many of us minimize the power of prayer and the spiritual works of mercy, fearing that they have not done enough corporal works of mercy. Jesus told St. Faustina:

I know, My daughter, that you understand it and that you do everything within your power. But write this for the many souls who are often worried because they do not have the material means with which to carry out an act of mercy. Yet spiritual mercy, which requires neither permissions nor storehouses, is much more meritorious and is within the grasp of every soul. If a soul does not exercise mercy somehow or other, it will not obtain mercy on the day of judgment. Oh, if only souls knew how to gather eternal treasure for themselves, they would not be judged, for they would forestall My judgment with their mercy (*Diary*, 1317).

Many of us remember as children learning about the spiritual and corporal works of mercy. The spiritual works call us to 1) admonish the sinner 2) instruct the ignorant 3) counsel the doubtful 4) comfort the sorrowful 5) bear wrongs patiently 6) forgive all injuries, and 7) pray for the living and the dead. The corporal works include 1) to feed the hungry 2) give drink to the thirsty 3) clothe the naked 4) ransom the captive 5) shelter the homeless 6) visit the sick, and 7) bury the dead. We should try to do at least one work of mercy every day.

As we heal from the battles of life and continue our spiritual journey, we must let others know of His unfathomable mercy. We are to be the light of the world, spreading the Good News of His great mercy. *"Let your light so shine before men, that they may see your good works and give glory to your Father who is in heaven"* (Mt 5:16). We must show love and mercy to all, not just those in our social class or to whom we will benefit socially or financially. *"For I tell you, unless your righteousness exceeds that of the Scribes and Pharisees, you will never enter the kingdom of heaven."* (Mt 5:20). We should strive to comfort the hurting through corporal and spiritual works of mercy, reminding those in need that only He can bring true and lasting peace. We are to be the heart, hands and feet of Jesus, radiating the merciful love of The Divine Mercy to a hurting world.

O Lord, give us the courage to ask for Your mercy and strength to be merciful to others. Help us become a beacon with bright light, guiding others in an unsettled and troubled world back to You, who are Love and Mercy itself.

Induction Ceremony

The intent of this ceremony is to formally recognize Eucharistic Apostles of The Divine Mercy members who have persevered, and to further bind them as a cohesive group. We pray that they will continue to deepen their understanding of the Mercy of God, and work together to build up the local church and spread the Good News.

Celebrant: Every ministry that we undertake flows from our baptismal call to live as Christ lived, to love as He loved, and to serve as He served. As you prepare to deepen your response to ministry by joining this outreach ministry, I invite you to light your candle at this time.

Questions and Answers:	Celebrant or lay leader
Do you reject Satan?	Candidate: I do.
And all his works?	Candidate: I do.
And all his empty promises?	Candidate: I do.

Do you believe in God, the Father Almighty, creator of heaven and earth?

Candidate: I do.

Do you believe in Jesus Christ, his only Son, our Lord, who was born of the Virgin Mary, was crucified, died, and was buried, rose from the dead, and is seated at the right hand of the Father?

Candidate: I do.

Do you believe in the Holy Spirit, the holy Catholic Church, the communion of saints, the forgiveness of sins, the resurrection of the body, and life everlasting?

Candidate: I do.

Do you believe that God is Love and Mercy itself?

Candidate: I do.

Do you believe that God loves and forgives even the greatest sinner?

Candidate: I do.

Do you believe that Jesus Christ is present, Body and Blood, Soul and Divinity in the Eucharist?

Candidate: I do.

This is our faith; this is the faith of the Church. We are proud to profess it, in Christ Jesus our Lord!

Candidate: Amen.

Members: Almighty and Eternal God, through the intercession of Mary, Mother of the Eucharist and Mother of Mercy Itself, I, _____, freely and in full awareness, dedicate myself as a member of the Eucharistic Apostles of The Divine Mercy. I firmly desire to participate in its spiritual benefits, which through the Divine Mercy are obtained by the works of all its members. I promise to live the Mission of the Eucharistic Apostles of The Divine Mercy, going about my daily tasks, submitting them to the will of God, and trusting in His great goodness. I shall faithfully strive to follow the Guidelines for Daily Living, including a strong prayer life and a firm conviction to better learn the faith and build up the local Church through spiritual and corporal works of mercy.

Celebrant: (or Lay Facilitator if priest not available) I affirm that you are called to be ambassadors of Christ and vessels of His great mercy. You are called in a stronger way to be witnesses to everyone of His great mercy and His True Presence in the Blessed Sacrament. You are to be the hands and feet of Jesus, bringing in the lost sheep from the highways and byways. You are to do these works out of love for God and in thankfulness of His great mercy for us all.

All: For the Grace to Be Merciful to Others (*Diary*, 163)

O Most Holy Trinity! As many times as I breath, as many times as my heart beats, as many times as my blood pulsates through my body, so many thousand times do I want to glorify Your mercy.

I want to be completely transformed into Your mercy and to be Your living reflection, O Lord. May the greatest of all Your attributes, that of Your unfathomable mercy, come to pass through my heart and soul to my neighbor.

Help me, O Lord, that my eyes may be merciful, so that I may never suspect or judge from appearances, but look for what is beautiful in my neighbors' souls and come to their rescue.

Help me, that my ears might be merciful, so that I might give heed to my neighbors' needs and not be indifferent to their pains and moanings.

Help me, O Lord, that my tongue may be merciful, so that I may never speak negatively of my neighbor, but have a word of comfort and forgiveness for all.

Help me, O Lord, that my hands may be merciful and filled with good deeds, so that I may do only good to my neighbors and take upon myself the more difficult and toilsome tasks.

Help me, that my feet may be merciful, so that I may hurry to assist my neighbor, overcoming my own fatigue and weariness. My true rest is in the service of my neighbor.

Help me, O Lord, that my heart may be merciful, so that I myself will feel all the sufferings of my neighbor. I will refuse my heart to no one. I will be sincere even with those who, I know, will abuse my kindness. And I will lock myself up in the most merciful heart of Jesus. I will bear my own sufferings in silence. May Your mercy, Lord, rest upon me.

You Yourself command me to exercise the three degrees of mercy. The first: the act of mercy, of whatever kind. The second: the word of mercy – if I cannot carry out a work of mercy, I will assist by my words. The third: prayer – if I cannot show mercy by deeds or words, I can always do so by prayer. My prayer reaches out even there where I cannot reach out physically.

O my Jesus, transform me into Yourself for You can do all things. AMEN.

Miracles of the Eucharist

Lanciano, 700 AD

Lanciano is a small coastal town on the Adriatic Sea in Italy. The term means "the lance," and Tradition has it that Saint Longinus, the soldier whose lance pierced the heart of Jesus from which flowed Blood and Water (Jn 19:34) was from Lanciano. Longinus converted after the events of the crucifixion and was eventually martyred for the faith.

At the time of this Eucharistic miracle, heresy was spreading in the Church about the True Presence of Our Lord in the Eucharist. A monk was having doubts and his doubts were growing stronger. One morning during Mass at the Consecration, he began to shake and tremble and faced the people to show them what had happened.

The Host had turned to Flesh and the wine into Blood!

This miracle took place nearly 1300 years ago and is ongoing. In the 1970s testing was done and revealed the flesh to be human heart tissue and the blood of human origin, both AB blood type. The blood had characteristics of living blood and no preservatives of any kind were found in either specimen. We ponder the miracle of Lanciano and Sacred Scripture:

So Jesus said to them, *"Very, truly, I tell you, unless you eat the Flesh of the Son of Man and drink His Blood, you have no life in you: Those who eat My Flesh and drink My Blood have eternal life, and I will raise them up on the last day"* (Jn 6:53:54).

Excite in us hunger and thirst for Your Eucharistic food, Lord, so that in following You and tasting Your heavenly bread, we may come to enjoy eternal life.

Adapted with permission from Eucharistic Miracles *by Joan Cruz, 1987, Tan Books and Publishers.*

Bologna, 1333

This miracle took place in 1333 in Bologna, Italy, and occurred because a pious young girl of eleven had a burning desire to receive Our Lord in the Eucharist.

Imelda Lambertini was born of wealth and her father was Count Eagno Lambertini. She entered the Dominican Convent at age nine and was loved by the older nuns. She had a burning love at a very young age for Jesus in the Eucharist and wanted to receive Communion but was unable because she was not the required twelve years of age.

The Lord gave her a special gift on the Feast of the Ascension in 1333. While praying, a Host appeared suspended in mid-air in front of her. The priest was called and he gave her Holy Communion. She went into ecstasy and never awakened. She died while receiving her First Holy Communion!

Devotion to Blessed Imelda began and in the early 1900s a community of Dominicans was started called the Dominican Sisters of the Blessed Imelda. They strive to spread love for the Eucharist and encourage Perpetual Adoration. Blessed Imelda's incorrupt body lies in the church of San Sigismondo near the University of Bologna. Pope St. Pius X named her Protectress of First Holy Communicants.

O Lord, let us die to You daily and receive You in the Eucharist as if it were our last. Let us also become as little children, having that innocent love and complete childlike trust in Your love and mercy.

Adapted with permission from personal communication and literature from Rev. Don Giulo Melaguti, Rettore di S. Sigismondo, Via S. Sigismondo 7, Bologna, Italy.

Santarem, 1247

A woman whose husband was unfaithful sought advice from a sorceress who promised he would change his ways if the woman brought her a Consecrated Host. The sorceress told her to feign an illness, so she could receive Communion during the week and bring her the Host. The woman knew this was wrong, but went to Communion and did not consume Our Lord. She left Mass and on the way to the sorceress, the Host began to bleed. Several people noticed and thought the woman was bleeding. Fear overcame her and she went home and put the Host in a trunk, wrapped in her handkerchief and covered with clean linen.

During the night she and her husband were awakened by a bright light coming from the trunk which illuminated the room. Angels had opened the trunk and freed Our Lord from the handkerchief. The wife told her husband of the incident and that the trunk contained a Consecrated Host. Both spent the night on their knees in adoration. A priest was called and took the Host back to the church and sealed it in melted beeswax.

Nineteen years later a priest opened the tabernacle and noticed the wax container had broken and the Host sealed in a crystal pyx. The miracle, 750 years old in 1997, was celebrated with much festivity in Santarem.

We may ask why the Lord gives us these miracles and perhaps it is to show how present He is in the Eucharist and how much He loves us. He desires that all of us, even the lost sheep, come back to the fold and that He loves us, even when we sin. He is the God of Mercy and Love, and wants us to share that Love and Mercy with others.

Adapted with permission from The Study and Story of the Relics and Eucharistic Miracle of Santarem *by Carlos Evaristo; 1992.*

PART TWO: DAILY PRAYERS AND PRACTICES

Recommended Daily Prayers and Practices

As Eucharistic Apostles of the Divine Mercy, prayer will be an important part of your life and increased spirituality. Attendance at daily Mass is suggested if the responsibilities of your state in life permit. Daily recitation of the Rosary and Divine Mercy Chaplet is encouraged. Also, members of the Eucharistic Apostles of The Divine Mercy should read daily from Sacred Scripture and readings on Divine Mercy, preferably from the *Diary of Saint Faustin*a or Pope John Paul II's Encyclical, *The Mercy of God*. To this end, we have the following suggestions and recommendations to enhance your prayer life.

Sunday: Thank God for blessings and trials received and ask for strength in efforts for family unification. Recall and reflect on the Resurrection of Our Lord. Read from Sacred Scripture and reflect on how to apply it to daily life.

Monday: Pray to the Holy Spirit asking for His gifts of love, wisdom, and fortitude in our daily walk. Read Sacred Scripture, especially from Acts of the Apostles, and meditate on the power of the Holy Spirit.

Tuesday: Ask the angels to intercede for the members of the ministry and families. Read on the lives of the Saints and ponder their lives and how we are all called to be Saints.

Wednesday: Honor St. Joseph and ask him to intercede for all fathers to better understand the gift of fatherhood and its responsibilities. Read from Sacred Scripture and reflect on the beauty of fatherhood, life, and families.

Thursday: Pray for an increased devotion to the Holy Eucharist, and ask that Our Lord's guiding light descend upon all members and families of the Eucharistic Apostles of The Divine Mercy. Pray especially for all priests that they grow in fervor and zeal for Our Lord. Read from Sacred Scripture, the *Diary of Saint Faustina*, or from the section on Eucharistic Miracles in the prayer book.

Friday: Offer reparation to His Sacred Heart for all offenses and pray for an increased First Friday devotion. Read from Sacred Scripture, from Pope John Paul II's Encyclical on Divine Mercy, or from the *Diary of Saint Faustina*.

Saturday: Honor Our Lady and pray for increased devotion to her Immaculate Heart and the spreading of First Saturday devotions. Read from Sacred Scripture, especially Luke 1:39-56, selected prayers, or from any of the writings of St. Louis de Montfort, reflecting on his motto "to Jesus through Mary." It is also recommended that you make a monthly confession, especially on the first Saturday of each month.

Other readings and prayers are recommended if they follow Church teaching and if they promote the beauty of our Catholic faith.

Other Special Recommendations

We recommend daily recitation of the Divine Mercy Chaplet, as well as daily recitation of the Most Holy Rosary.

How to Pray The Divine Mercy Chaplet

The Divine Mercy Chaplet is to be prayed, in addition to daily devotion, hourly in Eucharistic Adoration Chapels for the sick and dying.

The Chaplet may be prayed using ordinary Rosary Beads. You may begin the Chaplet with the following introductory prayers:

"You expired, Jesus, but the source of life gushed forth for souls, and the ocean of mercy opened up for the whole world. O Fount of Life, unfathomable Divine Mercy, envelop the whole world and empty Yourself out upon us" (*Diary,* 1319).

"O Blood and Water, which gushed forth from the Heart of Jesus as a fount of Mercy for us, I trust in You" (3 times) (*Diary*, 187).

Then say these prayers:

Our Father, who art in heaven, hallowed be Thy name; Thy kingdom come; Thy will be done on earth as it is in heaven. Give us this day our daily bread, and forgive us our trespasses as we forgive those who trespass against us. Lead us not into temptation but deliver us from evil. Amen.

Hail Mary, full of grace, the Lord is with you. Blessed are you among women, and blessed is the fruit of your womb, Jesus. Holy Mary, Mother of God, pray for us sinners, now and at the hour of our death. Amen.

I believe in God, the Father almighty, Creator of heaven and earth, and in Jesus Christ, his only Son, our Lord, who was conceived by the Holy Spirit, born of the Virgin Mary, suffered under Pontius Pilate, was crucified, died, and was buried; he descended into hell; on the third day he rose again from the dead; he ascended into heaven, and is seated at the right hand of God the Father almighty; from there he will come to judge the living and the dead. I believe in the Holy Spirit, the holy catholic Church, the communion of saints, the forgiveness of sins, the resurrection of the body, and life everlasting. Amen.

Then on the "Our Father" beads, say the following words:

"Eternal Father, I offer You the Body and Blood, Soul and Divinity of Your dearly beloved Son, Our Lord Jesus Christ, in atonement for our sins and those of the whole world."

On the "Hail Mary" beads, say the following words;

"For the sake of His sorrowful Passion, have mercy on us and on the whole world."

In conclusion, after the five decades, say these words three times:

"Holy God, Holy Mighty One, Holy Immortal One, have mercy on us and on the whole world."

The Holy Rosary

The Rosary should be prayed daily, if possible.

The Joyful Mysteries: 1) The Annunciation of the Archangel Gabriel to the Virgin Mary; 2) The Visitation of the Virgin Mary to the Parents of St. John the Baptist; 3) The Birth of Our Lord at Bethlehem; 4) The Presentation of Our Lord at the Temple; and 5) The Finding of Our Lord in the Temple.

The Sorrowful Mysteries: 1) The Agony of Our Lord in the Garden of Gethsemane; 2) The Scourging of Our Lord at the Pillar; 3) The Crowning of Our Lord with Thorns; 4) The Carrying of the Cross by Our Lord to Calvary; and 5) The Crucifixion and Death of Our Lord.

The Glorious Mysteries: 1) The Resurrection of Our Lord from the Dead; 2) The Ascension of Our Lord into Heaven; 3) The Descent of the Holy Spirit upon the Apostles; 4) The Assumption of Our Blessed Lady into Heaven; and 5) The Coronation of Our Blessed Lady as Queen of Heaven and Earth.

The Mysteries of Light: 1) Baptism of the Lord; 2) The Wedding Feast at Cana; 3) Jesus proclaims the coming of the Kingdom of God.; 4) The Transfiguration; and 5) Institution of the Eucharist.

PART THREE: WEEKLY CENACLE FORMATION SCHEDULE

Schedule for Weeks 1-50

Week One — Theme: Ministry Overview

READING ASSIGNMENT TO PREPARE FOR THIS WEEK:

This is our first week, and members will read the Cenacle Formation Manual article, "Overview of the Message of Divine Mercy." It reviews:

• The Image of Jesus, The Divine Mercy and the signature "Jesus, I Trust In You"
• The Divine Mercy Chaplet
• The Feast Day of Divine Mercy
• The virtue of trust

Our God has unfathomable mercy to offer each and every one of us if we will open our hearts and souls to His action, but we must trust in Him.

LEARNING AND DISCUSSION:

1) What is one way you have noticed God's mercy in your life?
2) What does it mean to trust in Jesus? (as in, "Jesus, I Trust in You")
3) Reflect on how you might spread Divine Mercy in your workplace

LESSON GOALS:

At the end of the discussion, members should understand:

• What the rays in the image represent,
• The promises associated with recitation of The Divine Mercy Chaplet and the Feast of Divine Mercy,
• Why trust is paramount to living the message of Divine Mercy.

Week Two — Theme: The Divine Mercy Chaplet and the Eucharist

READING ASSIGNMENT TO PREPARE FOR THIS WEEK:

Cenacle Formation Manual: "The Divine Mercy Chaplet and Eucharistic Adoration"
Scripture — Jn 6:48-56;
Catechism — Paragraphs (#) 1366, 1394, 1397

WEEK OVERVIEW:

Throughout the formation process, we will be learning and praying more about God's Divine Mercy. The Chaplet of Divine Mercy, an Eucharistic prayer, is a means of devotion to the Mercy of God. Jesus Christ is the Bread of Life, and made a sacrifice for us once and for all by dying on the Cross. This sacrifice is re-presented each time the Liturgy of the Eucharist is celebrated.

LEARNING AND DISCUSSION:

1) How is the Chaplet a Eucharistic prayer?
2) Why is it important to pray the Chaplet for the sick and dying? (*Diary*, 687 and 811)
3) How is it possible that the Chaplet applies the death of Christ to the sufferings we meet every day?
4) How can those in the health-related professions use the Chaplet?

Para 684, 834

LESSON GOALS:

At the end of the discussion, members should understand:

• How The Divine Mercy Chaplet is a Eucharistic prayer,
• The importance of reciting the Chaplet hourly for the sick and dying, particularly in Adoration Chapels worldwide.

Week Three — Theme: About Saint Faustina

READING ASSIGNMENT TO PREPARE FOR THIS WEEK:

Cenacle Formation Manual: Article entitled "Saint Faustina: A Model for Eucharistic Apostles of The Divine Mercy,"

(For an in-depth view of the life and spirituality of Saint Faustina, the book *The Life of Faustina Kowalska: The Authorized Biography* by Sister Sophia Michalenko, CMGT is recommended.)

WEEK OVERVIEW:

   This week an overview of the life of Saint Faustina is discussed. The Lord used this simple, holy nun from Poland to spread the message of His great love and mercy. She had only a third-grade education, yet her writings reflect a deep spirituality and mystical union with God.

LEARNING AND DISCUSSION: *of the Most Blessed Sacrement*

1) What title did Saint Faustina add to her name? (*Diary*, 3)
2) Why does the Lord often manifest His greatest works in the poor, uneducated, young, etc.? (*Diary*, 464)
3) What can we learn from Saint Faustina in living our lives?

LESSON GOALS:

   At the end of the discussion, members should understand:

• Why the Lord often chooses the weakest for His greatest works,
• We are all called to be apostles of mercy, including the family and workplace
• The promises given to her regarding those that spread the message of His mercy.

Week Four — Theme: The Image of Divine Mercy

READING ASSIGNMENT TO PREPARE FOR THIS WEEK:

Cenacle Formation Manual: "The Image and Feast Day"
Diary, (entries) 47-49, 299, 313, 327, 341, 414.

WEEK OVERVIEW:

This discussion centers on the Image of The Divine Mercy and its associated promises. The Lord requested that the Image be venerated worldwide.

LEARNING AND DISCUSSION:

1) What do the rays represent? (*Diary*, 299)
2) Why is it important to receive the Sacraments of Mercy (Eucharist and Reconciliation) frequently?
3) What issues in daily life can keep us from accepting graces from His mercy? Why should we have an Image in the home and office?

LESSON GOALS:

At the end of the discussion, members should understand:

- How the rays in the Image represent the Eucharist and Baptism/Penance (Sacraments of Mercy) and the need for a sacramental life,
- The importance of trust in all situations, and in immersing ourselves in His rays of mercy and love.

Week Five — Theme: The Feast of Divine Mercy

READING ASSIGNMENT TO PREPARE FOR THIS WEEK:

Cenacle Formation Manual: "The Image and Feast Day"

WEEK OVERVIEW:

The Feast of Divine Mercy, celebrated specifically at the Lord's request, is discussed, including preparation and the promises associated with it.

LEARNING AND DISCUSSION:

1) When is the Feast Day? How can we spread knowledge of this great day? (*Diary*, 49)
2) What are the promises associated with it? (*Diary*, 300)
3) What did the Holy Father declare about the Feast Day on Mercy Sunday 2000?

LESSON GOALS:

At the end of the discussion, members should understand:

• When the Feast of Mercy is celebrated,
• How to prepare for the Feast and the promises associated with it.

Week Six — *Diary*, 46-60

READING ASSIGNMENT TO PREPARE FOR THIS WEEK:

Scripture — Prov 3:5
Catechism — #145, 1816

WEEK OVERVIEW:

This week begins a series of readings from the *Diary* of Saint Faustina. Although certain points and key entries are mentioned, other sentences may touch a member's heart, and that member should feel free to bring them up in the discussion. The Image of The Divine Mercy and the virtues required to live the message are discussed.

LESSON AND DISCUSSION:

1) Where does Jesus want the Image venerated? (*Diary*, 47)
2) How does distrust on the part of souls make Jesus feel? (*Diary*, 50) How can we use this point to assist others in dealing with problems?
3) What traits are important for graces to flow? (*Diary*, 55)

LESSON GOALS:

At the end of the discussion, members should understand:

• A better understanding of the promises associated with the Image of The Divine Mercy,
• The importance of trust, simplicity, and humility in our daily life.

Week Seven — *Diary*, 61-68

READING ASSIGNMENT TO PREPARE FOR THIS WEEK:

Scripture — Mk 14:32-36
Catechism — #164, 1508, 1521

WEEK OVERVIEW:

The readings discuss Saint Faustina's sufferings and her attitudes towards daily trials. The importance and necessity of suffering, as well as the grace the Lord gave her to handle trials, is reviewed.

LEARNING AND DISCUSSION:

1) How did the Lord assist her when draining potatoes? (*Diary,* 65)
2) Was Saint Faustina a suffering soul? (*Diary,* 67)
3) What should our attitude be on suffering? How can we help others deal with suffering?

LESSON GOALS:

At the end of the discussion, members should understand:

• The role of suffering in life and what our disposition toward these trials should be,
• The need to ask for God's grace and to follow Him in His footsteps, as we try to offer up our sufferings up for the salvation of souls, and the glorification of the Kingdom of God.

Week Eight — *Diary*, 69-78

READING ASSIGNMENT TO PREPARE FOR THIS WEEK:

Scripture — Mt 6:7-8; Eph 6:10-12
Catechism — #2732-2733

WEEK OVERVIEW:

The lesson discusses Saint Faustina's doubts, her periods of spiritual darkness, and temptation. We all go through similar periods in life, and the importance of a sacramental life is paramount in overcoming these obstacles.

LEARNING AND DISCUSSION:

1) How did the Lord reassure her? (*Diary,* 74)
2) Did Saint have doubts? Did she have temptation? (*Diary*, 77)
3) How can we assist each other in resisting temptation?

LESSON GOALS:

At the end of the discussion, members should understand:

• Doubts, anxieties, and fears will occur in our own lives; we must pray for a deeper trust in God,
• Periods of dryness will occur, and we must pray for the grace of perseverance in prayer to get through these difficult periods.

Week Nine — *Diary*, 79-91

READING ASSIGNMENT TO PREPARE FOR THIS WEEK:

Scripture — 2 Tim 4:6-8
Catechism — #967-970

WEEK OVERVIEW:

The lesson deals with the importance of effort and suffering, and that the Lord rewards for effort, and not results. The vision of the rays coming from the Monstrance is also discussed, as well as consecration to Our Lady.

LEARNING AND DISCUSSION:

1) Does the Lord reward for results? (*Diary*, 86, 90)
2) Why is Holy Communion and Adoration important and what emanated from His Heart? (*Diary*, 87, 91) Think of examples in which the rays of mercy emanated through you and out to others in the last week.
3) Saint Faustina asks for Mary's intercession *(Diary*, 79); how is Mary our Mother in the order of grace?

LESSON GOALS:

At the end of the discussion, members should understand:

- The necessity of receiving Holy Communion frequently and praying in front of Our Lord in Eucharistic Adoration,
- How Our Lady is the Church's model of faith and charity, as well as the close relationship that Saint Faustina had with Our Blessed Mother.

Week Ten — Mary, Mother of Mercy and the Eucharist

READING ASSIGNMENT TO PREPARE FOR THIS WEEK:

Cenacle Formation Manual Article: "Mary, Mother of Mercy"
Scripture — Jn 19:26-27; Lk 1:46
Catechism — #964, 967, 969
Diary, 449, 805

WEEK OVERVIEW:

The lesson focuses on Mary, Mother of Mercy and Mother of the Eucharist. She is the perfect role model and wants to bring us closer to her Son, Jesus.

LEARNING AND DISCUSSION:

1) How can we imitate Mary's inseparable union with Christ? How are the Sacraments wells of grace and strength to accomplish this?
2) Why is Mary the perfect model for all Christians?
3) Why is consecration to Our Blessed Mother so important in today's world in our journey to the Lord?
4) In Church-approved apparitions, Mary always points to the Eucharistic Jesus and the sacraments. Have we followed her pleas? (Increased Mass attendance and reception of the sacraments?)

LESSON GOALS:

At the end of the discussion, members should understand:
• An emphasis on Our Lady's role as our spiritual mother: her gift to us from Christ, her inseparable union with Christ, her courage under the cross.
• Consideration of her example of obedience to the Word of God; a model of faith, hope, and charity for us to follow.

Week Eleven — *Diary*, 92-93

READING ASSIGNMENT TO PREPARE FOR THIS WEEK:

Scripture — Jas 3:3-5; 1 Pet 5:5
Catechism — #2445-2447

WEEK OVERVIEW:

The readings bring to light the tongue and how great faults are committed by it. The religious vows of poverty, chastity, and obedience are reviewed. Spiritual poverty and materialism in society are good discussion points.

LEARNING AND DISCUSSION:

1) Why did St. Faustina ask for a healing of the tongue? (*Diary*, 92)
2) What is spiritual poverty and can people with little means lack it?
3) How did the tongue get you or a coworker in trouble since the last meeting?

LESSON GOALS:

At the end of the discussion, members should understand:

• How we should use our tongue only to proclaim the Good News, looking at ourselves and seeing how often we fail in this,
• How the corporal works of mercy are the expression of God's love in our lives, as all are called to be the hands and feet of Jesus.

Week Twelve — *Diary*, 94-98

READING ASSIGNMENT TO PREPARE FOR THIS WEEK:

Scripture — Mt 16:24
Catechism — #2729-2731

WEEK OVERVIEW:

A discussion on the interior life, including spiritual dryness, despair, temptations, and distractions are discussed. The readings are rich in spirituality, and should be read slowly, carefully, and with much introspection.

LEARNING AND DISCUSSION:

1) What is spiritual dryness? (*Diary*, 96)
2) Why is perseverance so important? (*Diary*, 97)
3) How were you tested in the last week?

LESSON GOALS:

At the end of the discussion, members should understand:

- That we are on a spiritual journey, and that times of spiritual dryness exist,
- The importance of persevering in times of dryness, as well as abandoning oneself to deeper trust in God,
- The importance of trials in life.

Week Thirteen — *Diary*, 99-112

READING ASSIGNMENT TO PREPARE FOR THIS WEEK:

Scripture — Jn 6:48-50
Catechism — #1333-1336, 1394

WEEK OVERVIEW:

Saint Faustina writes of great sufferings and trials, as well as the mystical experiences of her soul. The writings speak of deep suffering, yet God sustained her through all her trials. Her love of the Eucharist, the food for her spiritual journey, is noteworthy.

LEARNING AND DISCUSSION:

1) Did Saint omit Communion in spite of all her sufferings? (*Diary*, 105)
2) How did God sustain her through these sufferings? (*Diary*, 111)
3) What sufferings did you encounter or witness recently?

LESSON GOALS:

At the end of the discussion, members should understand:

- That in times of trial one should battle against fear letting trust in God dominate the soul,
- Holy Communion is the spiritual nourishment for our journey; it is the pinnacle of our Faith.

Week Fourteen — *Diary*, 112-115

READING ASSIGNMENT TO PREPARE FOR THIS WEEK:

Scripture — Num 5:6-7
Catechism — #1422, 1430-1433, 1485-1490

WEEK OVERVIEW:

The writings discuss Saint Faustina's experiences with spiritual confessors but also speak for the need for sincerity and openness in the confessional, the need for obedience and humility, as well as one's journey to personal holiness.

LEARNING AND DISCUSSION:

1) Discuss Saint's comment, "A magnificent building will never rise if we reject the insignificant bricks" (*Diary*, 112).
2) What words of advice did she give to the soul striving for sanctity regarding the Sacrament of Reconciliation? (*Diary*, 113)
3) In what small ways could you have recently acted differently at home or work?

LESSON GOALS:

At the end of the discussion, members should understand:

• A deeper appreciation of the gift of the Sacrament of Reconciliation and why sincerity and openness in the confessional is important,
• The quest for personal holiness requires that we pay attention to our minor imperfections, focusing on ourselves and not on the faults of others.

Week Fifteen — Theme: Be Merciful
as Your Father is Merciful

READING ASSIGNMENT TO PREPARE FOR THIS WEEK:

Scripture — Lk 16:19-31; Lk 18: 35-43; Jas 2:17
Catechism — #1822, 1826, 1829
Diary, 742, 1316, 1317, 692

WEEK OVERVIEW:

The theme for this week is mercy, and a number of Scripture, *Diary*, and Catechism entries are quoted. The spiritual and corporal works of mercy are the expression of God's love in us. Efforts in building up the local church should be part of the group discussion.

LEARNING AND DISCUSSION:

1) What are the spiritual and corporal works of mercy?
2) What are some of the needs of our family and friends?
3) How can the group build up the local church? How can you better build up your family or those at work?

LESSON GOALS:

At the end of the discussion, members should understand:

• The spiritual and corporal works of mercy and some of the needs of the local church,
• The importance of exercising mercy in our daily lives through small deeds of mercy, as well as being more sensitive to those around us.

Week Sixteen — Theme: Mary, Mother of Mercy

READING ASSIGNMENT TO PREPARE FOR THIS WEEK:

Cenacle Formation Manual Article: "Our Lady of Guadalupe and Mother of Mercy"
Catechism — #2270-2272, 2276-2279

WEEK OVERVIEW:

The readings focus on our Blessed Mother, who is the Mother of Mercy and Mother of the Eucharist. The Seven Sorrows of Mary are also detailed. Also, the role of Our Lady in stopping the human sacrifice in Mexico in the 16th century and the need for her intercession in stopping the culture of death today is discussed.

LEARNING AND DISCUSSION:

1) Discuss Our Lady of Guadalupe, human sacrifice, abortion, and euthanasia.
2) What were the "Seven Sorrows of Mary?"
3) During trials and suffering, where are we to fix our gaze? In what ways have you found trust in God difficult?

LESSON GOALS:

At the end of the discussion, members should understand:

- The apparition of Our Lady to Juan Diego in 1531 and the need for her intercession today in stopping the culture of death,
- Seven sorrows of Our Lady and the need for us to fix our gaze on Our Lord in times of trial.

Week Seventeen — Theme: Trust

READING ASSIGNMENT TO PREPARE FOR THIS WEEK:

Cenacle Formation Manual Article: "Trust"
Scripture — Ps 56:1-3; Prov 3:5; Lk 5:5-7
Catechism — #1820-1821

WEEK OVERVIEW:

This week's readings focus on Trust, the hallmark of the message of Divine Mercy. Various Scripture, Catechism, and *Diary* quotes are used to emphasize the importance of letting God be in control of our daily lives.

LEARNING AND DISCUSSION:

1) When in life do we need to turn things over to God and trust?
2) Why is trust easier for a humble person?
3) When do we need trust the most? (*Diary*, 1777).

LESSON GOALS:

At the end of the discussion, members should understand:

• A deeper understanding of how trust and fear are incompatible,
• How pride can rob us of the virtue of trust, due to lack of humility,
• Trust opens the door to many graces, which we then radiate out to other souls.

Week Eighteen — Theme: Sinners and My Mercy

READING ASSIGNMENT TO PREPARE FOR THIS WEEK:

Scripture — Mt 9:12-13
Catechism — #1030-1032
Diary, 723, 1146, 1275, 1396-97, 1521, 1541, 1602

WEEK OVERVIEW:

The theme for the week is mercy and sin, and various *Diary* quotes emphasize God's unfathomable mercy, especially towards the greatest sinner. We should remind ourselves that God's mercy is greater than our worst sin.

LEARNING AND DISCUSSION:

1) Who has the greatest right to His mercy? (*Diary*, 723)
2) What promise is given to priests who extol the mercy of God? (*Diary*, 1521)
3) Why is humility so important especially in the workplace? (*Diary*, 1602)

LESSON GOALS:

At the end of the discussion, members should understand:

• God's mercy is greater than our worst sin,
• God wants us to return to Him in humility through the Sacrament of Reconciliation,
• We never tire of proclaiming His mercy and priests should extol the mercy of God as hardened sinners will repent on hearing of His mercy.

Week Nineteen — Theme: Tell the World of My Mercy

READING ASSIGNMENT TO PREPARE FOR THIS WEEK:

Scripture — Acts 1:8
Catechism — #2013, 900-901
Diary, 301, 687, 998, 1142, 1074-75, 1190, 1521, 1540, 1588, 329

WEEK OVERVIEW:

The readings detail the call to evangelize the Good News of His great mercy, as well as the promises about those who extol and glorify His mercy.

LEARNING AND DISCUSSION:

1) What is the greatest attribute of God? (*Diary*, 301)
2) What about souls who glorify His mercy and how will Our Lord protect them? (*Diary*, 1075)
3) How can we better tell the people we encounter of God's mercy?

LESSON GOALS:

At the end of the discussion, members should understand:

• That mercy is the greatest attribute of God,
• The greatest sinner has the greatest right to His mercy,
• The promises given to souls who spread the honor of His mercy.

Week Twenty — Eucharistic Adoration
and The Divine Mercy Chaplet

READING ASSIGNMENT TO PREPARE FOR THIS WEEK:

Cenacle Formation Manual Article: "The Divine Mercy Chaplet and the Dying"

WEEK OVERVIEW:

The relationship of the Divine Mercy Chaplet, the Eucharist, and the Passion of Our Lord are discussed, as well as the importance of reciting the Chaplet in adoration chapels hourly for the sick and dying.

LEARNING AND DISCUSSION:

1) Is the Chaplet efficacious even if recited not at the bedside?
2) Does the Holy Father recommend Adoration?
3) How is the Eucharist related to the Passion?

LESSON GOALS:

At the end of the discussion, members should understand:

- The importance of recitation of The Divine Mercy Chaplet for the sick and dying in adoration chapels worldwide, if one's station in life permits,
- How The Divine Mercy Chaplet is a Eucharistic prayer,
- The promises the Lord gave Saint Faustina regarding The Divine Mercy Chaplet.

Week Twenty-one — *Diary*, 118-128

READING ASSIGNMENT TO PREPARE FOR THIS WEEK:

Scripture — Jn 13:34; Jas 1:26-27
Catechism — #2196

WEEK OVERVIEW:

The readings focus on the human tongue, and how we can use it to be critical and judgmental of others, or give glory to God. The readings should call us all to reflect on our interactions with others. The readings bring to light the fact that the tongue is a "small member but it boasts of big exploits" (Jas 3:5).

LEARNING AND DISCUSSION:

1) Do you tremble when you think about giving an account of your tongue? (*Diary*, 119)
2) Are we as demanding and judgmental of ourselves as we are of others? (*Diary*, 128)
3) Reflect on ways that you have fallen short since last meeting regarding use of the tongue

LESSON GOALS:

At the end of the discussion, members should understand:

• The need to be careful of how we use our tongue,
• That we need to avoid being judgmental and less exacting on others, focusing our energies instead on personal spiritual growth and development.

Week Twenty-two — *Diary*, 129-136

READING ASSIGNMENT TO PREPARE FOR THIS WEEK:

Scripture — Jn 15:18
Catechism — #2559, 2631, 2706

WEEK OVERVIEW:

The writings discuss that if we follow in Christ's footsteps we will be misunderstood, rejected, and humiliated. Satan will use our discouragement and anxiety to retard our spiritual growth. It is through our own misery that the Lord will show us His mercy.

LEARNING AND DISCUSSION:

1) Was Saint Faustina ever misunderstood and humiliated?
2) Why is humility so important for spiritual growth?
3) Were you misunderstood recently?

LESSON GOALS:

At the end of the discussion, members should understand:

- That following in His footsteps requires sacrifice and suffering,
- Humility is critical for spiritual growth, as it opens doors to receiving God's grace.

Week Twenty-three — *Diary*, 137-145

READING ASSIGNMENT TO PREPARE FOR THIS WEEK:

Scripture — Mt 10:12-13; Jn 14:27; Gal 5:22

Catechism — #736, 1832

WEEK OVERVIEW:

The readings focus on inner peace and discernment of God's will. Saint Faustina writes on pure love and inner peace and how her soul was in a state of great peace. The gifts of the Holy Spirit are also reviewed.

LEARNING AND DISCUSSION:

1) How can peace be helpful in discernment? (*Diary*, 143)

2) Is peace a fruit of the Holy Spirit?

3) How can we better find true peace for ourselves and others?

LESSON GOALS:

At the end of the discussion, members should understand:

- The need for being careful and testing one's inspirations, as well as the inner peace found in conforming to God's will,
- That pure love is capable of great deeds.

Week Twenty-four — *Diary*, 146-151

READING ASSIGNMENT TO PREPARE FOR THIS WEEK:

Scripture — Eph 6:10-20
Catechism — #2731, 2729

WEEK OVERVIEW:

The writings focus on the interior struggle of the soul, as well as the role of trust and suffering in spiritual advancement. Saint Faustina writes of a vision of St. Thérèse of the Child Jesus and of the importance of doing little things well in our daily lives.

LEARNING AND DISCUSSION:

1) What are the interior difficulties she writes about? (*Diary*, 147)
2) Can we trust and be afraid of suffering? (*Diary*, 149 and 151)
3) Saint Faustina had a dream about St. Thérèse of the Child Jesus. How can we do the little things in life in a more caring and loving way at home and at work?

LESSON GOALS:

At the end of the discussion, members should understand:

- The interior difficulties of discouragement, dryness, heaviness of spirit, temptation – and how to combat them through prayer and a sacramental life,
- The "little things" matter in our daily lives and we need to focus how to do them in a more loving and caring fashion.

Week Twenty-five — The Life of Saint Faustina

READING ASSIGNMENT TO PREPARE FOR THIS WEEK:

Cenacle Formation Manual Article: "The Life of St. Faustina."

LEARNING AND DISCUSSION:

1) What aspect of St. Faustina's life can you relate to your own?
2) What virtue or aspect of her life do you feel you can best incorporate into your life?

LESSON GOALS:

At the end of the discussion, members should understand:

• The heroic, virtuous life lived by Saint Faustina and how each of us is called to imitate her.
• How she made an ordinary life extraordinary – able to do even the simplest things for the greater glory of God.

Week Twenty-six — *Diary*, 152-162

READING ASSIGNMENT TO PREPARE FOR THIS WEEK:

Scripture — Mt 24:13; I Thess 5:12; Jn 6:52-58
Catechism — #2731, 2634-36, 264, 1402, 1416

WEEK OVERVIEW:

The readings include Saint Faustina's need for frequent Holy Communion and her desire that the Host reside in her always. Her soul was on fire as she reflected on the Holy Eucharist.

LEARNING AND DISCUSSION:

1) How am I to aid others and assist them in their spiritual journey? Did I have opportunities at home and at work?
2) What steps can I take to persevere in my prayer life?
3) How do I approach the reception of the Eucharist? Is my soul on fire like Saint Faustina's? (*Diary*, 160)

LESSON GOALS:

At the end of the discussion, members should understand:

• The power of intercession,
• The difficulties in prayer that we encounter,
• The deep spiritual nourishment we receive in Holy Communion.

Week Twenty-seven — *Diary*, 163-170

READING ASSIGNMENT TO PREPARE FOR THIS WEEK:

Scripture — 1 Pet 3:8-9; Lk 6:36; Phil 4:6-7
Catechism — #2447, 2304-5

WEEK OVERVIEW:

Saint Faustina's "Prayer to Be Merciful" is part of the week's readings, as well as her striving for inner peace through humility. Her desire to do works of mercy are also included.

LEARNING AND DISCUSSION:

1) How can I be merciful to my family on a daily basis?
2) How can the group build up the local church through corporal and spiritual works of mercy?
3) Is inner peace related to one's trust in God? (*Diary*, 169)

LESSON GOALS:

At the end of the discussion, members should understand:

• The need for mercy in our daily lives, to see Jesus in others, and to become aware of other's needs, both on a spiritual and corporal level,
• The need to be merciful toward others, particularly towards our family and coworkers, areas where we frequently have shortcomings.

Week Twenty-eight — *Diary*, 171-181

READING ASSIGNMENT TO PREPARE FOR THIS WEEK:

Scripture — Mt 4:18-22; Lk 12: 35-36; Ps 145:8; Lk 1:52
        Joel 2:12-13
Catechism — #2003, 2011, 2631

WEEK OVERVIEW:

Temptation, the Lord's flame of mercy, His attributes of holiness, justice, love, and mercy, and the need for humility to accept His grace are topics for the week.

LEARNING AND DISCUSSION:

1) How am I responding to God's call using the graces He has given me?
2) How does our humility make us more receptive to graces from God? In what ways were you called recently to show humility?
3) Do we ever get temptations during meditation? (*Diary*, 173)

LESSON GOALS:

At the end of the discussion, members should understand:

- How grace is given for the common good of the Church,
- How all our merits are pure grace from God,
- That forgiveness opens up our hearts to receive God's mercy and grace.

Week Twenty-nine — *Diary*, 182-196

READING ASSIGNMENT TO PREPARE FOR THIS WEEK:

Scripture — Mt 18:1-6; Rom 8:16-18; 2 Cor 12:7-9; Is 3:4-5

Catechism — #164, 2280-82

WEEK OVERVIEW:

A diversity of topics, including simplicity in life, the need to meditate on His Passion to better understand His love for us, and how our suffering can assist in the salvation of souls is discussed.

LEARNING AND DISCUSSION:

1) What is childlike trust? Why did Jesus come as a child? (*Diary*, 184)

2) What are the benefits of simplicity? In what ways do you find that difficult?

3) Why is it necessary to reflect on His Passion to better understand His mercy? How can our suffering help save souls? (*Diary*, 194)

LESSON GOALS:

At the end of the discussion, members should understand:

• The need for simplicity and humility in life, as well as a child-like trust,

• By meditating on His Passion, we will develop a deeper appreciation for the love burning in His heart for souls.

Week Thirty — Theme: Humility

READING ASSIGNMENT TO PREPARE FOR THIS WEEK:

Cenacle Formation Manual Article: "Humility"
Scripture — Phil 2:3; Col 3:12; 1Pet 5:5
Catechism — #525, 2559, 2631

WEEK OVERVIEW:

   Humility is a necessary virtue for spiritual growth. The weekly readings reiterate this in Sacred Scripture and the *Diary*. After reading the short chapter on humility, reflect on situations where pride did not allow one to practice the virtue of humility.

LEARNING AND DISCUSSION:

1) What keeps us from reconciling with people?
2) Why was Jesus born in a simple manger?
3) Did you encounter a humble person recently?

LESSON GOALS:

   At the end of the discussion, members should understand:

- How having the attitude of Mary, saying "let it be done to me according to Your word," should dominate our decision to get involved in the local church,
- How being judgmental is easy when we have spiritual pride,
- How reconciliation with others is easier if we practice humility.

Week Thirty-one — Theme: Forgiveness

READING ASSIGNMENT TO PREPARE FOR THIS WEEK:

Cenacle Formation Manual Article: "Forgiveness"

WEEK OVERVIEW:

Forgiveness, the virtue that opens the door to His mercy, is discussed in this week's lesson. Forgiveness and love will set us free, allowing us to "run the good race" (cf. 2 Tim 4:7). Many of us carry unresolved anger for years, and to better understand the great mercy of God, we must be forgiving of others, as He forgave us.

LEARNING AND DISCUSSION:

1) When do we most resemble God? (*Diary*, 1148)
2) Can lack of forgiveness cause problems later in life?
3) Why should we avoid being judgmental?
4) Did you have to ask for or forgive anyone recently?

LESSON GOALS:

At the end of the discussion, members should understand and appreciate:

• The role of forgiveness and living the message of Divine Mercy,
• That deeper healing will occur through forgiveness of others, opening our hearts to God's grace.

Week Thirty-two — Theme: Mercy

READING ASSIGNMENT TO PREPARE FOR THIS WEEK:

Cenacle Formation Manual Article: "Mercy"

WEEK OVERVIEW:

Mercy is love that seeks to lessen the misery of others. We are called to be merciful to others and to proclaim the mercy of God. The three ways of performing an act of mercy are discussed.

LEARNING AND DISCUSSION:

1) What is mercy and how can we be merciful on a daily basis?
2) What are the three ways of performing acts of mercy? (*Diary*, 742)
3) Discuss Mt 5:20, "Unless your righteousness exceeds the righteousness of the Scribes and Pharisees, you will by no means enter the kingdom of heaven."

LESSON GOALS:

At the end of the discussion, members should understand:

• The need for mercy from God in our own lives, as well as the need to merciful to others,
• That God came to heal the sick, not the healthy,
• The three ways of performing acts of mercy.

Week Thirty-three — Theme: Obedience

READING ASSIGNMENT TO PREPARE FOR THIS WEEK:

Cenacle Formation Manual Article: "Obedience"

WEEK OVERVIEW:

The virtues of obedience and humility are discussed, as well as the Lord's desire that obedience be practiced; that it is more important than long prayers and mortifications. He calls us to obedience, yet being obedient to Church teaching is at times difficult.

LEARNING AND DISCUSSION:

1) Why is it necessary to be obedient to Church teaching? (Prov 12:28)
2) How are the virtues of obedience and humility interrelated?
3) How are teachings on the gift of life beautiful, yet at times difficult? How is this difficult to live out in today's society?

LESSON GOALS:

At the end of the discussion, members should understand:

• God desires obedience more than burnt offering or sacrifice,
• Practice of obedience at times requires humility.

Week Thirty-four — Theme: The Hour of Mercy

READING ASSIGNMENT TO PREPARE FOR THIS WEEK:

Scripture — Jn 14:13-14; Mt 27;45-50
Diary, 1320, 1572

WEEK OVERVIEW:

The entries in the *Diary* regarding the Hour of Mercy are discussed, including the importance of reflecting on His Passion and love for us in that hour.

LEARNING AND DISCUSSION:

1) Why do we say The Divine Mercy Chaplet during the Hour of Mercy?

2) What are some of the promises connected with the Hour of Mercy? (*Diary*, 1320)

3) Did you encounter, receive, or share in God's mercy recently?

LESSON GOALS:

• At the end of the discussion, members should understand:
• When is the Hour of Mercy,
• The promises associated with the Hour of Mercy and The Divine Mercy Chaplet.

Week Thirty-five — Theme: Turn to Me for peace

READING ASSIGNMENT TO PREPARE FOR THIS WEEK:

Scripture — Mt 6:21; Jn 14:27
Catechism — #1427-1430
Diary, 300, 699, 1074, 1345, 1520

WEEK OVERVIEW:

The theme is peace and turning back to God, a conversion of the heart. The Lord told Saint Faustina that unless we turn to Him, we will not have peace. We are to approach the sea of mercy with great trust.

LEARNING AND DISCUSSION:

1) What are ways we attempt to satisfy the flesh, other than the Lord?
2) Reflect and discuss conversion of the heart and Ez 36:26-27.

LESSON GOALS:

At the end of the discussion, members should understand:

• The need for trust in order to obtain inner peace,
• That Jesus is calling us to a deeper conversion of heart.

Week Thirty-six — Theme: Reconciliation

READING ASSIGNMENT TO PREPARE FOR THIS WEEK:

Scripture — Num 5:6-7; Prov 28:13; Jn 20:21-23; 1Jn 1:9
Catechism — #1449-1450, 1458
Diary, 113, 377, 1760

WEEK OVERVIEW:

The Sacrament of Reconciliation is the theme for this discussion and requirements of the penitent and the formula of absolution reviewed. Frequent confession is suggested, as we obtain grace through the Sacrament.

LEARNING AND DISCUSSION:

1) What is the formula of absolution and what does penance require of the penitent? (Catechism, #1449-50)
2) Is confession of venial sins recommended? (Catechism, #1458)
3) What are the Sacraments of Mercy? How can we help educate fellow Catholics on the sacraments of mercy?

LESSON GOALS:

At the end of the discussion, members should understand:

• A deeper appreciation of the gift of the Sacrament of Reconciliation,
• The need for frequent confession and the graces received.

Week Thirty-seven — Eucharist, Trust, and Conversion

READING ASSIGNMENT TO PREPARE FOR THIS WEEK:

Cenacle Formation Manual Article: "Eucharist and Trust"

WEEK OVERVIEW:

The "Great Secret," the Eucharist, is discussed and how we are called to be the hands and feet of Jesus. We are to let Our Lord transfigure us into vessels of mercy, being a living reflection of Him. Trust in times of trial is made apparent through personal testimony.

LEARNING AND DISCUSSION:

1) How can we "live" the Eucharist?
2) What is the "Great Secret?"
3) In what ways did you act as an icon of mercy recently?

LESSON GOALS:

At the end of the discussion, members should understand:

• The need to live the Eucharist and be the light on a mountain-top to our fellow man,
• How the early Church understood the great gift of the Eucharist.

Week Thirty-eight — Conversation of the Merciful God with a Sinful Soul

READING ASSIGNMENT TO PREPARE FOR THIS WEEK:

Scripture — Lk 5:31-32; Lk 8:42-48
Diary, 1485

WEEK OVERVIEW:

The Lord's unfathomable mercy and love for us are highlighted in the readings. He knows we are nothing and of our wretchedness. He wants us to draw from the Fountain of Life.

LEARNING AND DISCUSSION:

1) Who makes the first move to establish relationship (the soul/God)?
2) How does the Lord want the soul to talk with Him?
3) What will Jesus give in return for all the soul's troubles and grief? Does He remember the soul's misery and sinfulness?

LESSON GOALS:

At the end of the discussion, members should understand:

- We are not to be afraid in coming to Him,
- His mercy is greater than the sins of the whole world,
- He wishes to heap upon us the treasures of His grace.

Week Thirty-nine — Conversation of the Merciful God with a Despairing Soul

READING ASSIGNMENT TO PREPARE FOR THIS WEEK:

Scripture — Prov 3:5; Lk 15:11-32
Catechism — #2091
Diary, 1486

WEEK OVERVIEW:

The readings for the week review conversations that the Lord has with a despairing soul, emphasizing the need for continued hope. The message of Divine Mercy is one of great hope, and at times we are all like the prodigal son, needing to keep coming back to Him and ask for His mercy. We should focus on His merciful Heart, and not be absorbed in our own misery.

LEARNING AND DISCUSSION:

1) What happens to the soul that spurns God's mercy?
2) How are we at times like the prodigal son, and why do we doubt God's unfathomable mercy?

LESSON GOALS:

At the end of the discussion, members should understand:

• That the message of Divine Mercy is a message of hope, understanding that God's mercy is greater than our sins, and His heart is filled with joy when, through conversion, we return to Him in humility,

• Our lack of trust wounds His heart more than all the sins we have committed.

Week Forty — Conversation of the Merciful God with a Suffering Soul

READING ASSIGNMENT TO PREPARE FOR THIS WEEK:

Scripture — Jn 12:24-26; Mt 5:44
Catechism — #1508
Diary, 1487

WEEK OVERVIEW:

The readings detail conversations of the Lord with a suffering soul. The Lord asks us not to lose heart, or give into despondency in times of trial. He tells us not to become discouraged, speaking to Him as a friend. He reminds us that there is no way to heaven except through the Way of the Cross.

LEARNING AND DISCUSSION:

1) How do we react to suffering and trials (anger, fear, etc.)? What is the shortest and surest way to heaven?
2) How does Jesus want us to converse with Him?
3) What is persecution a sign of? Why does God give us a share in suffering?

LESSON GOALS:

At the end of the discussion, members should understand:

• Suffering is a part of our life, and will become a source of our sanctification,
• The Lord gives us a share in His suffering because of His special love for us,
• Strength to bear sufferings comes from frequent reception of Holy Communion.

Week Forty-one — Conversation of the Merciful God with a Soul Striving after Perfection

READING ASSIGNMENT TO PREPARE FOR THIS WEEK:

Scripture — Mt 26:33-34, 26:69-75
Catechism — #1829, 2088
Diary, 1488

WEEK OVERVIEW:

He reminds the soul of the need to rely more on Him and that discouragement and an exaggerated anxiety are the greatest obstacles to holiness. Continued trust in Him in all situations is paramount.

LEARNING AND DISCUSSION:

1) In what ways do we daily fall into the same faults?
2) What are the greatest obstacles to holiness?

LESSON GOALS:

At the end of the discussion, members should understand:

• The continued need to trust in Him, and obstacles to holiness in our lives,
• How we deny Our Lord daily, yet He does not allot a certain number of pardons.

Week Forty-two — Conversation of the Merciful God with a Perfect soul

READING ASSIGNMENT TO PREPARE FOR THIS WEEK:

Scripture — Mt 6:19-21
Catechism — #1392, 1393
Diary, 1489

WEEK OVERVIEW:

The readings are a conversation with the Merciful God with a perfect soul. The Lord says that a single act of pure love pleases Him more than a thousand imperfect prayers, and that He will not give us anything beyond our strength. We are to be at peace, do our best, as He rewards for effort and not for results. Trust is the vessel by which we receive grace to do battle.

LEARNING AND DISCUSSION:

1) What did the Lord ask her to receive daily so as to get strength?

2) If a soul desires more mercy, how should it approach God? What is the key to receiving more grace? (*Diary*, 1578)

LESSON GOALS:

At the end of the discussion, members should understand:

• That Jesus is always with us, even if we don't feel His presence at the time,

• That small virtuous acts done out of love for Him have unlimited value in His eyes,

• Trust is the vessel by which we draw grace to do battle.

Week Forty-three — The Mercy of God

READING ASSIGNMENT TO PREPARE FOR THIS WEEK:

"On the Mercy of God" Encyclical: Chapter 1

WEEK OVERVIEW:

The world is in disarray and chaos, and many are crying out for the mercy of God. Many realize that their only hope is the mercy of God, and have found no satisfaction in the pleasures of the world. Not only are we to ask for His mercy and trust completely in Him, but we are to be merciful to others.

LEARNING AND DISCUSSION:

1) Why are people turning now to the mercy of God?

2) How does the concept of mercy cause uneasiness in man?

3) In what small ways can we daily show mercy?

LESSON GOALS:

At the end of the discussion, members should understand:

- All are in need of God's mercy, and that His mercy is greater than our shortcomings,
- That small acts of mercy can easily be done daily in the family and in the workplace, and will help heal wounds and build up the kingdom of God.

Week Forty-four — The Mercy of God

READING ASSIGNMENT TO PREPARE FOR THIS WEEK:

"On the Mercy of God" Encyclical: Chapter 4

WEEK OVERVIEW:

The parable of the Prodigal Son is discussed, and this story reminds us of our own shortcomings. At different points in our life we are like the prodigal son, the older brother, and the Father. Just as our loving Father wants us to return to Him and ask for forgiveness, we too are called to be as forgiving as the Father.

LEARNING AND DISCUSSION:

1) How are we at times like the prodigal son, and other times like the older brother?
2) Although the son had lost everything, what did he find when he returned to the Father?
3) How are we at times called to be like the Father?

LESSON GOALS:

At the end of the discussion, members should understand:

- At different times in our life, we are the Prodigal Son, the older brother, and the father,
- The Prodigal Son found everything when he returned home, something he had not found when living in the world.

Week Forty-five — The Mercy of God

READING ASSIGNMENT TO PREPARE FOR THIS WEEK:

"On the Mercy of God" Encyclical: Chapter 7

WEEK OVERVIEW:

The Church professes and proclaims mercy on the local level by bringing people to a more personal relationship with Jesus, and by its members living the love of God through the corporal works of mercy. The Sacrament of Reconciliation is active participation in His mercy. An understanding of His mercy leads to a deeper conversion. We realize there is no need for shame, guilt, and doubt; only trust in Him.

LEARNING AND DISCUSSION:

1) How does the Church profess and proclaim mercy on the local level?
2) How is participation in the Sacrament of Reconciliation a participation in mercy?
3) How does discovering God's mercy lead each of us to a deeper personal conversion?

LESSON GOALS:

At the end of the discussion, members should understand:

• That the Sacrament of Reconciliation enables us to participate in His mercy, which is greater than any sin we can commit,

• That trust in His mercy is the vessel by which we draw grace; through the Sacrament of Reconciliation we are forgiven and there is no need for shame, doubt, guilt and despair.

Week Forty-six — Theme: Trust

READING ASSIGNMENT TO PREPARE FOR THIS WEEK:

Scripture — 2 Mac 8:18; Is 12:2
Catechism — # 1814 - 1816
Diary, 723, 1059, 1074, 1273, 1520, 1578, 1777, 1784

WEEK OVERVIEW:

Trust is the hallmark of living the message of Divine Mercy, and is the vessel by which we draw grace. The more a soul trusts, the more grace it receives. Trust enables a soul to achieve great sanctity quickly. As disciples of Christ, we must not only keep the faith and live it, but profess it, and confidently bear witness to it.

LEARNING AND DISCUSSION:

1) How does the Lord desire that souls distinguish themselves? (*Diary*, 1578)

2) How can great sinners achieve great sanctity quickly? (*Diary*, 1784)

3) In what small ways can we share with others about God's mercy?

LESSON GOALS:

At the end of the discussion, members should understand:

• The need to trust completely in His mercy in all situations,

• A soul can achieve great sanctity quickly if it will only trust,

• Whoever places his trust in the mercy of God will be filled with divine peace at the hour of death.

Week Forty-seven — *Diary*, 197-217

READING ASSIGNMENT TO PREPARE FOR THIS WEEK:

Scripture — Mk 5:25-34
Catechism — #1503, 1511, 1523-1524

WEEK OVERVIEW:

The Lord asked St. Faustina to look into the abyss of His mercy, giving praise and glory to Him. He desires to give Himself to souls, and asked St. Faustina to go through the whole world and bring fainting souls to Him on the Feast of Divine Mercy, so that He can heal and strengthen them. The Anointing of the Sick, as well as giving Viaticum are topics also discussed.

LEARNING AND DISCUSSION:

1) What was Saint Faustina instructed to do with sinners? (*Diary*, 206)
2) A dying relative (*Diary*, 207) did not receive the Anointing of the Sick and Viaticum. Discuss these sacraments.

LESSON GOALS:

At the end of the discussion, members should understand:

• The Sacrament of the Anointing of the Sick and Viaticum,
• The need to celebrate the Feast of Divine Mercy, and to bring as many souls as possible to Him on that day.

Week Forty-eight — *Diary*, 218-230

READING ASSIGNMENT TO PREPARE FOR THIS WEEK:

Scripture — Is 43:25; Jn 20:21-23; 1 Jn 3:16-17

Catechism — #1429, 1436, 1443-1445, 1861

WEEK OVERVIEW:

In the readings for the week the Lord requests of Saint Faustina that she remain deeply at peace, letting nothing frighten or disconcert her. The reality of mortal sin is reviewed, as well as the need for conversion, and assisting our neighbor in need.

LEARNING AND DISCUSSION:

1) What should be our disposition towards life's struggles? (*Diary*, 219)
2) Saint Faustina was preparing for Confession (*Diary*, 225). What is mortal sin and why do we need the Sacrament of Reconciliation?
3) How can we help our brothers and sisters in need?

LESSON GOALS:

At the end of the discussion, members should understand:

- How we at times let anxiety and fear take control of our lives,
- Mortal sin, and what is does to the soul,
- How we can better assist our brothers and sisters in need, building up the local church.

Week Forty-nine — *Diary*, 231-240

READING ASSIGNMENT TO PREPARE FOR THIS WEEK:

Scripture — Mt 7:1-5; 2 Mac 12:46; 1 Cor 2:15
Catechism — #1030-1032

WEEK OVERVIEW:

Readings of the week focus on being judgmental of others, and how our judgements are often inaccurate and unjust. The Church teaching on the existence of purgatory and the poor souls in purgatory is reviewed.

LEARNING AND DISCUSSION:

1) Do we judge others in our daily interactions? (*Diary*, 236)
2) Saint Faustina mentioned purgatory (*Diary*, 240). What is the Church's teaching on purgatory?
3) In what ways were you judgmental recently?

LESSON GOALS:

At the end of the discussion, members should understand:

• How we must not be not be judgmental of others, reflecting on how we often fail in this regard,
• The existence of purgatory, as well as the need to pray for the poor souls n purgatory.

Week Fifty — Induction Ceremony as Eucharistic Apostles

See "Induction Rite" in this manual. If possible, do after Mass with the local priest/Spiritual Mentor presiding. The intent of this ceremony is to formally recognize Eucharistic Apostles of The Divine Mercy members who have persevered, and to further bind them as a cohesive group. We pray that they will continue to deepen their understanding of the Mercy of God, and work together to build up the local church and spread the Good News.

Permissions/Bibliography

Cruz, Joan Carroll, *Eucharistic Miracles*. Copyright © 1987. Tan Books and publishers, Inc., Rockford, IL 81104.

Division of Christian Education of the National Council of the Churches of Christ in the U.S.A. New revised Standard Version Bible. Copyright © 1987.

Kowalska, Faustina M., Saint. *Diary: Divine Mercy in my Soul.* Copyright © 1987 Congregation of Marians of the Immaculate conception. Marian Press, Stockbridge, MA 01263.

Libreria Editrice Vaticana. *Catechism of the Catholic Church* for the United States of America English translation. Copyright © 1994 United States Catholic Conference, Inc. Ligouri Publications, One Ligouri Drive, Ligouri, MO 63057-9999

Order of Saint Benedict, Inc. *Order for the Solemn Exposition of the Holy Eucharist,* Minister's Edition. Copyright © 1993 The Liturgical Press, Collegeville, MN 56321.

John Paul II, Pope, *The Mercy of God* (*Dives in Misericordia*) Encyclical Letter. English translation from the Vatican. Daughters of Saint Paul. Pauline Books & Media, 50 Saint Paul's avenue, Boston, Massachusetts 02130.

Valeriano, Don Antonio, *Nican Mopohua* translated in English by Rev. Réal Bourque, O.M.I., Box 717, Lowell, MA 01853.

All pictures of Eucharistic Miracles are used with permission.

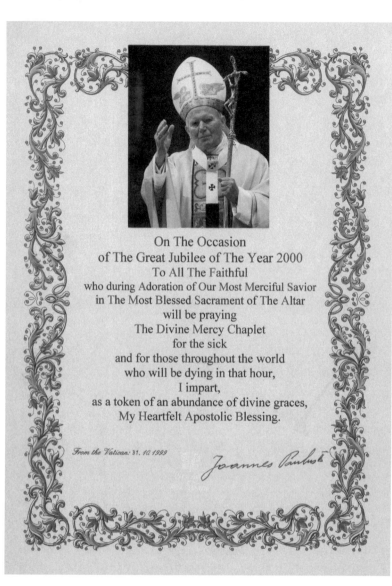

On The Occasion
of The Great Jubilee of The Year 2000
To All The Faithful
who during Adoration of Our Most Merciful Savior
in The Most Blessed Sacrament of The Altar
will be praying
The Divine Mercy Chaplet
for the sick
and for those throughout the world
who will be dying in that hour,
I impart,
as a token of an abundance of divine graces,
My Heartfelt Apostolic Blessing.

From the Vatican: 31. 10. 1999

Joannes Paulus II

Calling to Remembrance

the participation in Our Lord's Agony in Gethsemani of
Saint Maria Faustina Kowalska of The Most Blessed Sacrament,
who at least thrice in her lifetime willingly accepted the violent pains
that convulsed her for three hours and at times caused her to lose consciousness,
as allowed by Jesus in order to offer reparation to God
for infants murdered in their mothers' wombs (Diary, §1276),

To All Members of

The Eucharistic Apostles of The Divine Mercy
—A Lay Ministry Outreach of the Congregation of Marians
of The Immaculate Conception of the Most Blessed Virgin Mary—

and

To All The Faithful Worldwide, who join them in offering

The Divine Mercy Chaplet

— revealed to St. M. Faustina for averting divine chastisement —
for mothers, that they not abort their offspring;
for infants in danger of being put to death in the womb;
for a change of heart of providers of abortions and of their collaborators;
for human victims
of stem cell research, genetic manipulation, cloning and euthanasia;
and for all entrusted with the government of peoples,
that they may promote the "Culture of Life"
so as to put an end to the "culture of death,"

I impart,
as a token of a Superabundance of Divine Graces,
My Heartfelt Apostolic Blessing.

Given at the Vatican, March, A.D. 2003,
Solemnity of the Incarnation of The Divine Word
In the 25th year of My Pontificate

Joannes Paulus